110667165

From the monument in Westminster Abbey

WILLIAM COLLINS

From an engraving after a drawing made at the age of 14

The Poems of
GRAY *and* COLLINS

Edited by
AUSTIN LANE POOLE

London
OXFORD UNIVERSITY PRESS
New York Toronto

Oxford University Press, Amen House, London **E.C.4**

GLASGOW NEW YORK TORONTO MELBOURNE WELLINGTON
BOMBAY CALCUTTA MADRAS KARACHI KUALA LUMPUR
CAPE TOWN IBADAN NAIROBI ACCRA

First edition (in the Oxford
  Standard Authors)   1919
Second edition   1927
Third edition   1937
Reprinted 1941, 1948, 1950, 1957, 1959 *and* 1961

PRINTED IN GREAT BRITAIN
O.S.A.

HUGH STEPHENS LIBRARY
STEPHENS COLLEGE
COLUMBIA, MISSOURI

PR
3500
.A5
P6
1937

POEMS

OF

THOMAS GRAY

EDITED BY

AUSTIN LANE POOLE

103566

PREFACE TO THE THIRD EDITION

Mr. Austin Lane Poole, who was responsible for this edition of the *Poems of Thomas Gray* when it was first published in 1917, has for many years been occupied in medieval studies and did not wish to undertake the work of revision, which is now considered necessary. The plan of his edition, which is still followed, was to print the poems from the best available texts, to prefix to each poem a note stating the source from which the text was derived, what manuscripts, if any, are extant, and giving details of its first publication. Notes are added at the end of the book to record the most important variants in Gray's manuscripts or in transcripts from his manuscripts. The original version of the Elegy is printed in an Appendix and a second Appendix discusses Gray's removal from Peterhouse to Pembroke College.

For the purpose of his work Mr. Poole was given access to the Gray manuscripts at Pembroke College, Cambridge, and at Eton College, and he expressed his gratitude to the Master and Fellows of Pembroke and to Mr. C. H. Blakiston, Keeper of the Memorial Buildings at Eton. He also acknowledged his obligation to the late Dr. Walker and Professor Temperley, of Peterhouse, for information concerning Gray's departure from the College, and to the late Sir Edmund Gosse for assistance.

In the present, as in the 1917 edition, the text of the ten poems printed in Dodsley's edition of 1768 is followed, as the book was published with Gray's authority and under his instructions. Three other poems were printed in

Gray's lifetime: the *Long Story* in the edition of *Six Poems* with Bentley's Designs (1753); the *Ode performed at the Installation of the Duke of Grafton as Chancellor of the University* printed by the University for the ceremony in 1769; and the verses *On Lord Holland's Seat near Margate*. These verses appeared anonymously, and certainly without Gray's consent, in *The New Foundling Hospital for Wit* (1769).

The posthumous poems are printed, some from Gray's manuscripts in his Commonplace Book or from Gray's letters to Mason, in which they were included; some from copies made by Mason, Wharton, or Dyce, of manuscripts of Gray's, which cannot now be traced, some from printed versions of Mason, Walpole, Gosse, or others.

In the present revision some of the poems have been printed from texts of better authority than those which were followed in Mr. Poole's edition. The introductory matter, the notes prefixed to the poems, and the notes on the text of the poems have been corrected and revised, in the light of researches undertaken in the last ten years. Many corrections are based on notes or appendixes in the recently published *Correspondence of Thomas Gray* edited by Paget Toynbee and Leonard Whibley (3 vols., Oxford, 1935). This book is cited as *Correspondence* in the notes, and references to individual letters are to the letters as numbered in it.

The process of revision has been supervised by Mr. Leonard Whibley.

November 1936.

CONTENTS OF GRAY'S POEMS

ILLUSTRATIONS

THE CHIEF EDITIONS

ODE ON A DISTANT PROSPECT OF ETON COLLEGE. Printed for Dodsley, London, 1747 (a folio pamphlet, 8 pp.).

DODSLEY'S COLLECTION OF POEMS BY SEVERAL HANDS. London, 1748. Second edition, 1748. (Containing *Ode on the Spring, Ode on the Death of a Favourite Cat,* and *Ode on a Distant Prospect of Eton College.*)

AN ELEGY WROTE IN A COUNTRY CHURCH YARD. London, printed for R. Dodsley in Pall Mall; 1751.

DESIGNS BY MR. R. BENTLEY FOR SIX POEMS BY MR. T. GRAY. London, 1753. (See facsimile of title-page, p. 99. It contained the *Ode on the Spring, Ode on the Death of a Favourite Cat, Ode on a Distant Prospect of Eton College,* the *Hymn to Adversity,* the *Elegy,* and the *Long Story.*)

ODES. Strawberry Hill, 1757. (Containing the two Pindaric Odes, *The Progress of Poesy* and *The Bard.* This was the first book to be printed by Horace Walpole's Press at Strawberry Hill.)

POEMS BY MR. GRAY. London: printed for J. Dodsley in Pall Mall, 1768. (See facsimile of title-page, p. 15. This was the first Collected Edition.)

POEMS BY MR. GRAY. Glasgow: Printed by Robert and Andrew Foulis, Printers to the University. 1768. (Issued with Gray's consent from Beattie's transcript, the notes being added on the final pages.)

POEMS BY MR. GRAY. Dublin: Printed by William Sleater in Castle Street. 1768. (This includes *The Long Story.*)

POEMS BY MR. T. GRAY. Cork: William Flyn. 1768. (This and the previous book are of interest as they appeared in the original year of publication.)

ODE PERFORMED IN THE SENATE HOUSE AT CAMBRIDGE, JULY 1, 1769, AT THE INSTALLATION OF HIS GRACE AUGUSTUS-HENRY FITZROY, DUKE OF GRAFTON, CHANCELLOR OF THE UNIVERSITY. Cambridge, 1769.

THE POEMS OF MR. GRAY, to which are prefixed Memoirs of his Life and Writing, by W. Mason. York, 1775.

Poems by Mr. Gray. A new Edition. London, 1778. (With a short life, and Gray's will.)

Poems with Notes, by Gilbert Wakefield. London, 1786.

Poetical Works. Ed. Stephen Jones. London, 1799 and 1800.

The Works of Thomas Gray, by Mason, to which are sub-joined extracts Philological, Poetical, and Critical, from the author's original manuscripts, selected and arranged by T. J. Mathias. 2 vols. London, 1814.

Poems, with Life, Notes, and an Essay on his Poetry by Rev. J. Mitford. London, 1814, 1816, and 1836.

Poetical Works. Ed. Moultrie, with a life by Mitford. Eton, 1847.

Works. Ed. Gosse. 4 vols. London, 1884.

Elegy. From the MS. Ed. Sir W. Fraser. London, 1884.

Elegy. Text of the First Quarto with variant readings. Ed. F. G. Stokes. Oxford, 1929.

Poetical Works. Aldine Edition, with Introduction, Life, Notes, and a Bibliography by J. Bradshaw. London, 1891.

English Poems. Ed. D. C. Tovey. Cambridge, 1904.

Letters of Thomas Gray. Ed. D. C. Tovey, 3 vols. London, 1900–12.

The Correspondence of Gray, Walpole, West, and Ashton. Ed. Paget Toynbee. 2 vols. Oxford, 1915.

Correspondence of Thomas Gray. Ed. Paget Toynbee and Leonard Whibley. 3 vols. Oxford, 1935.

THE EDITION OF 1768

Gray's instructions to Dodsley have been preserved, and the MS. is now in the British Museum : it opens as follows :

' Let the Title be only *Poems by Mr Gray* without any mention of notes or additions. you will judge, whether what few notes there are should stand at bottom of each page, or be thrown to the end. all I desire is, that the text be accurately printed, & therefore whoever corrects the press, should have some acquaintance with the Greek, Latin, & Italian, as well as the English, tongues. let the order stand thus, unless you have begun to print already : if so, it is indifferent to me.

　1. Ode. (Lo, where the rosy-bosom'd &c:)
　2. Ode, on the death of a favourite Cat.

3. Ode, on a distant prospect of Eton-College.
4. Ode, to Adversity.
5. The progress of Poesy, a Pindaric Ode.
6. The Bard, a Pindaric Ode.
7. The Fatal Sisters.
8. The Descent of Odin.
9. The Triumphs of Owen, a fragment.
10. Elegy, written in a country-churchyard.

You will print the four first & the last from your own large edition (first publish'd with M^r B:^s plates) in the 5th & 6th you will do well to follow the edition printed at St: y-hill: I mention this, because there are several little faults of the press in your Miscellanies.   remember, the *Long Story* must be quite omitted. now for the notes.'

The notes follow, and one misprint of Dodsley's edition which escaped Gray can be corrected from them: in the opening note to *The Fatal Sisters* (page 79) ' Valhalla ' is misprinted ' Valkalla ', owing to a slight ambiguity in the shaping of the *h*. The correction is important, as the *Oxford English Dictionary* refers to this note as the first appearance of the word in literary English.   Folios 5 to 9 contain the Norse poems. After the last note on the *Elegy* there are final instructions :

'I hope, you have not begun to reprint: but if you have, you must throw the notes, &c: to the end, or where you please, omitting the mottoes, wch do not much signify.

When you have done, I shall desire you to present in my name a copy to Mr Walpole in Arlington-street, another to Mr Daines Barrington (he is one of the Welch Judges) in the Inner-Temple; & a third to M^r *J: Butler at Andover :* whether this latter Gentleman be living or not, or in that neighbourhood, I am ignorant : but you will oblige me in making the enquiry. if you have no better means of knowing, a line directed to the Post-mistress at Andover will bring you information. after this you may (if you please) bestow another copy or two on me. I am

Your obed^t humble Servant

T. GRAY.

P:S: It is *Mr Foulis of Glasgow*, that prints them in Scotland : he has been told, that you are doing the same. I have desired, he would not print a great number, & could wish the same of you.'

THE CHIEF MANUSCRIPTS

GRAY'S COMMONPLACE BOOK, 3 vols., now at Pembroke College, Cambridge, in which Gray transcribed most of his poems. The poems in Gray's autograph are: *Ode on the Spring*, the Eton Ode, *Sonnet on the Death of Richard West*, *Ode on the Death of a Favourite Cat*, *Hymn to Adversity*, *The Progress of Poesy*, *The Fatal Sisters*, *The Descent of Odin*, *The Triumphs of Owen*, the *Elegy*, *A Long Story*, *The Alliance of Education and Government*, *The Death of Hoel*. At the end of the third volume of the Commonplace Book Mason transcribed the following poems from Gray's papers: *Ode on the Pleasure arising from Vicissitude*, *Fragment of a Hymn to Ignorance*, *Song* [1], *Song* [2], *Tophet*, *Stanzas to Mr. Bentley*, *Epitaph on Sir W. P. Williams*, *Sketch of his own Character*.

THE ETON MSS., now at Eton College, in Gray's autograph:
(1) *Ode on a Distant Prospect of Eton College*, (2) the first draft of the *Elegy*.

THE WHARTON MS.=Egerton MS. 2400 of the British Museum, consisting of Gray's letters to Wharton, with autograph copies of some poems, and transcripts of others made by Wharton. The autograph poems are the Ode on the Cat (ff. 19*b*, 20), *The Alliance of Education and Government*, ll. 1–57, completed by Wharton (ff. 29*b*, 30), the *Elegy* (ff. 45–6), *The Progress of Poesy* (ff. 67–8), *The Bard*, ll. 57–144 (ff. 75–6), *Parody on an Epitaph* (f. 181). The verses *On Lord Holland's Seat near Margate* (f. 232) and some 'Impromptus' are in Wharton's hand.

ADDITIONAL MS. 38511 of the British Museum, consisting of Gray's instructions to Dodsley for printing the *Poems* of 1768, and including the text of the Norse Poems (see pp. 9–10).

ADDITIONAL MSS. 32561 and 32562 of the British Museum, being Volumes III and IV of the Commonplace Books of John Mitford. The second of these contains Mitford's notes and transcripts of the poems in a rougher form; the first is his fair copy.

CHRONOLOGICAL TABLE

CONTAINING THE PRINCIPAL EVENTS IN GRAY'S LIFE

A.D.	ÆT.	
1716		Thomas Gray born, December 26, in Cornhill, where his mother, Dorothy Gray, kept a shop in partnership with her sister, Mary Antrobus. His father, Philip Gray, was a scrivener by profession. Thomas was the only survivor of a family of twelve. [Richard West born.]
1717		[Horace Walpole born.]
1725		[William Mason born.]
c.1725	c.9	Entered Eton, where his uncles, Robert and William Antrobus, were Assistants. He formed ' the quadruple alliance ' with Richard West, Horace Walpole, and Thomas Ashton.
1734	17	Entered as pensioner at Peterhouse, July 4; admitted October 9.
1735	18	Admitted at Inner Temple, November 22. [Horace Walpole entered at King's, West at Christ Church.]
1738	21	Left Cambridge without taking his degree, intending to read for the Bar at the Inner Temple.
1739	22	Accompanied Horace Walpole on a Continental tour. Sailed from Dover March 29 (N.S.); spent April and May at Paris and the next three months at Rheims ; was at Lyons in September. On the way to Geneva, visited the Grande Chartreuse ; crossed the Mont Cenis, arriving at Turin November 7. By Genoa and Bologna to Florence, where he spent the winter at the house of Horace Mann.
1740	23	Visited Rome (March) and Naples (June); returned to Florence July 7.
1741	24	Left Florence for Venice ; at Reggio quarrelled with Walpole and proceeded to Venice. Returned through Padua, Verona, Milan, Turin, and Lyons.

A.D.	ÆT.	
		Again visited the Grande Chartreuse and wrote an Alcaic Ode in the Visitors' Book of the Monastery. Reached London in September. (For account of his travels, see Letters 59–97.) Philip Gray died, November 6. Gray began his first English poem, the fragmentary *Agrippina*.
1742	25	[Richard West died, June 1.] Gray wrote the *Ode on the Spring*, *Ode on a Distant Prospect of Eton College*, *Sonnet on the Death of Richard West*, the *Hymn to Adversity*, and the *Hymn to Ignorance* (fragment). Returned to Peterhouse as a fellow commoner (October). Gray's chief friends at Cambridge were Thomas Wharton, Fellow of Pembroke till his marriage in 1747, James Brown, afterwards Master of Pembroke, and William Mason. Mrs. Gray and her sister, Mary Antrobus, settled with a third sister, Anna, the widow of Jonathan Rogers, at Stoke Poges in Buckinghamshire.
1743	26	Graduated as LL.B.
1745	28	Reconciled with Horace Walpole.
1747	30	Wrote the *Ode on the Death of a Favourite Cat*.
1748	31	Gray's house in Cornhill burnt down. Began the *Alliance of Education and Government*.
1749	32	[William Mason elected Fellow of Pembroke, partly through Gray's influence.] Gray's aunt, Mary Antrobus, died.
1750	33	Completed the *Elegy*; wrote the *Long Story*.
1753	36	Gray's mother died. Gray visited Wharton at Durham.
1754	37	During this and the two following years Gray was engaged with the Pindaric Odes. *The Progress of Poesy* (begun in 1752) was finished in 1754 and *The Bard* in 1757.
1756	39	Moved from Peterhouse to Pembroke Hall, March 5 (see Appendix).
1757	40	Was offered, but refused, the post of Poet Laureate, vacant through the death of Colley Cibber.
1759	42	Took lodgings in Southampton Row in order to be

A.D.	ÆT.	
		near the British Museum, which was opened to the public in January.
1761	44	Returned to Cambridge in December; wrote *The Fatal Sisters*, the *Descent of Odin*, and the *Welsh Odes*.
1762	45	Made the acquaintance of Norton Nicholls. Visited Mason at York and Wharton at Old Park, and made a tour of places of interest in the north. Dr. Turner, Regius Professor of Modern History, died. Gray made overtures for the post, but Lord Bute gave it to Laurence Brockett.
1764	47	Visited Southampton, Salisbury, &c.
1765	48	Visited Scotland; stayed at Glamis Castle, where he met James Beattie.
1766	49	Travelled in Kent.
1767	50	Stayed at Old Park and Hartlepool. First visit to the Lakes.
1768	51	Stayed in Kent. Wrote verses *On Lord Holland's Seat near Margate*. Appointed Regius Professor of Modern History.
1769	52	Composed the *Ode for Music* to be performed at the Installation of the Duke of Grafton, Chancellor of the University. Visited the Lakes (see the journal of his tour which he sent to Wharton in *Correspondence*, vol. iii, 1074 ff.).
1770	53	Made an excursion through the Western Counties in company of Norton Nicholls.
1771	54	Taken ill suddenly while dining at Pembroke and died a week later, July 30. He was buried beside his mother in the Churchyard at Stoke Poges.

POEMS

BY

Mr. GRAY.

LONDON:

Printed for J. DODSLEY, in Pall-mall.

MDCCLXVIII.

ODE

ON THE

SPRING.

[The MS. copy in Gray's Commonplace Book at Pembroke College, Cambridge, is entitled 'Noontide, an Ode', and is dated 'at Stoke, the beginning of June, 1742. Sent to Fav· not knowing he was then Dead'. Favonius was Gray's name for Richard West. The Ode was first published anonymously in 1748 in the first edition of Dodsley's *Collection of Poems by Several Hands*, ii. 265.]

O D E

ON THE

S P R I N G.

Lo ! where the rosy-bosom'd Hours,
Fair VENUS' train appear,
Disclose the long-expecting flowers,
And wake the purple year !
The Attic warbler pours her throat,
Responsive to the cuckow's note,
The untaught harmony of spring :
While whisp'ring pleasure as they fly,
Cool Zephyrs thro' the clear blue sky
Their gather'd fragrance fling   10

Where'er the oak's thick branches stretch
A broader browner shade ;
Where'er the rude and moss-grown beech
O'er-canopies the glade,*

*   ————a bank
            O'ercanopied with luscious woodbine.
                            Shakesp. Mids. Night's Dream.

Beside some water's rushy brink
With me the Muse shall sit, and think
(At ease reclin'd in rustic state)
How vain the ardour of the Crowd,
How low, how little are the Proud,
How indigent the Great !   20

Still is the toiling hand of Care :
The panting herds repose :
Yet hark, how thro' the peopled air
The busy murmur glows !
The insect youth are on the wing,
Eager to taste the honied spring,
And float amid the liquid noon * :
Some lightly o'er the current skim,
Some shew their gayly-gilded trim
Quick-glancing to the sun † .   30

To Contemplation's sober eye ‡
Such is the race of Man :

---

* " Nare per æstatem liquidam————"
                                        Virgil. Georg. lib. 4.
†   ————sporting with quick glance
   Shew to the sun their waved coats drop'd with gold.
                                Milton's Paradise Lost, book 7.
‡ While insects from the threshold preach, &c.
                                M. GREEN, *in the Grotto.*
                      Dodsley's Miscellanies, Vol. V. *p.* 161.

And they that creep, and they that fly,
Shall end where they began.
Alike the Busy and the Gay
But flutter thro' life's little day,
In fortune's varying colours drest :
Brush'd by the hand of rough Mischance,
Or chill'd by age, their airy dance
They leave, in dust to rest.   40

Methinks I hear in accents **low**
The sportive kind reply :
Poor moralist ! and what art thou ?
A solitary fly !
Thy Joys no glittering female meets,
No hive hast thou of hoarded sweets,
No painted plumage to display :
On hasty wings thy youth is flown ;
Thy sun is set, thy spring is gone——
We frolick, while 'tis **May**.   50

O D E

ON THE DEATH OF A

FAVOURITE CAT,

Drowned in a Tub of Gold Fishes.

[Two copies of this poem exist in Gray's handwriting : (1) in a letter to Wharton, March 17, 1747, and (2) among the Pembroke MSS. It was first published in Dodsley's *Collection*, 1748 (first edition), ii. 267.]

O   D   E

ON THE DEATH OF A

FAVOURITE CAT,

Drowned in a Tub of Gold Fishes.

'Twas on a lofty vase's side,
Where China's gayest art had dy'd
  The azure flowers, that blow ;
Demurest of the tabby kind,
The pensive Selima reclin'd,
  Gazed on the lake below.

Her conscious tail her joy declar'd :
The fair round face, the snowy beard,
  The velvet of her paws,
Her coat, that with the tortoise vies,   10
Her ears of jet, and emerald eyes,
  She saw ; and purr'd applause.

Still had she gaz'd ; but 'midst the tide
Two angel forms were seen to glide,
    The Genii of the stream :
Their scaly armour's Tyrian hue
Thro' richest purple to the view
    Betray'd a golden gleam.

The hapless Nymph with wonder saw:
A whisker first and then a claw,   20
    With many an ardent wish,
She stretch'd in vain to reach the prize.
What female heart can gold despise ?
    What Cat's averse to fish ?

Presumptuous Maid ! with looks intent
Again she stretch'd, again she bent,
    Nor knew the gulf between.
(Malignant Fate sat by, and smil'd)
The slipp'ry verge her feet beguil'd,
    She tumbled headlong in.   30

Eight times emerging from the flood
She mew'd to ev'ry watry God,
    Some speedy aid to send.
No Dolphin came, no Nereid stirr'd :
Nor cruel *Tom*, nor *Susan* heard.
    A Fav'rite has no friend !

From hence, ye Beauties, undeceiv'd,
Know, one false step is ne'er retriev'd,
 And be with caution bold.
Not all that tempts your wand'ring eyes   40
And heedless hearts, is lawful prize ;
 Nor all, that glisters, gold.

O D E

DISTANT PROSPECT

OF

ETON COLLEGE.

Ἄνθρωπος· ἱκανὴ πρόφασις εἰς τὸ δυστυχεῖν.

MENANDER.

[The Pembroke MS. is entitled ' Ode. on a distant Prospect of Windsor, & the adjacent Country ', and is dated ' at Stoke, Aug. 1742 '. The autograph MS. preserved at Eton College has the same title, except that ' distant ' is omitted; the envelope which contained it has the interesting note that the MS. belonged to Wordsworth, to whom it was given by the Rev. W. Dixon, Mason's nephew. The Ode was the first of Gray's English productions to appear in print, being published anonymously in a folio pamphlet by Dodsley in 1747. Dodsley also included it in his *Collection of Poems*, 1748 (first edition), ii. 261.]

O D E

ON A DISTANT PROSPECT OF

ETON COLLEGE.

Ye distant spires, ye antique towers,
That crown the watry glade,
Where grateful Science still adores
Her HENRY's * holy Shade;
And ye, that from the stately brow
Of WINDSOR's heights th' expanse below
Of grove, of lawn, of mead survey,
Whose turf, whose shade, whose flowers among
Wanders the hoary Thames along
His silver-winding way.   10

   Ah happy hills, ah pleasing shade,
Ah fields belov'd in vain,
Where once my careless childhood stray'd,
A stranger yet to pain!

   * King HENRY the Sixth, Founder of the College.

I feel the gales, that from ye blow,

A momentary bliss bestow,

As waving fresh their gladsome wing,

My weary soul they seem to sooth,

And,* redolent of joy and youth,

To breathe a second spring.   20

   Say, Father THAMES, for thou hast seen

Full many a sprightly race

Disporting on thy margent green

The paths of pleasure trace,

Who foremost now delight to cleave

With pliant arm thy glassy wave ?

The captive linnet which enthrall ?

What idle progeny succeed

To chase the rolling circle's speed,

Or urge the flying ball?   30

   While some on earnest business bent

Their murm'ring labours ply

'Gainst graver hours, that bring constraint

To sweeten liberty :

Some bold adventurers disdain

The limits of their little reign,

---

  * And bees their honey redolent of spring.
               Dryden's Fable on the Pythag. System.

And unknown regions dare descry :
Still as they run they look behind,
They hear a voice in every wind,
And snatch a fearful joy.   40

   Gay hope is theirs by fancy fed,
Less pleasing when possest ;
The tear forgot as soon as shed,
The sunshine of the breast :
Theirs buxom health of rosy hue,
Wild wit, invention ever-new,
And lively chear of vigour born ;
The thoughtless day, the easy night,
The spirits pure, the slumbers light,
That fly th' approach of morn.   50

   Alas, regardless of their doom,
The little victims play !
No sense have they of ills to come,
Nor care beyond to-day :
Yet see how all around 'em wait
The Ministers of human fate,
And black Misfortune's baleful train !
Ah, shew them where in ambush stand
To seize their prey the murth'rous band !
Ah, tell them, they are men !   60

These shall the fury Passions tear,
The vulturs of the mind,
Disdainful Anger, pallid Fear,
And Shame that sculks behind;
Or pineing Love shall waste their youth,
Or Jealousy with rankling tooth,
That inly gnaws the secret heart,
And Envy wan, and faded Care,
Grim-visag'd comfortless Despair,
And Sorrow's piercing dart.   7c

Ambition this shall tempt to rise,
Then whirl the wretch from high,
To bitter Scorn a sacrifice,
And grinning Infamy.
The stings of Falshood those shall try,
And hard Unkindness' alter'd eye,
That mocks the tear it forc'd to flow;
And keen Remorse with blood defil'd,
And moody Madness * laughing wild
Amid severest woe.   80

Lo, in the vale of years beneath
A griesly troop are seen,

*   ——Madness laughing in his ireful mood.
                Dryden's Fable of Palamon and Arcite.

The painful family of Death,
More hideous than their Queen :
This racks the joints, this fires the veins,
That every labouring sinew strains,
Those in the deeper vitals rage :
Lo, Poverty, to fill the band,
That numbs the soul with icy hand,
And slow-consuming Age.   90

   To each his suff'rings : all are men,
Condemn'd alike to groan,
The tender for another's pain ;
Th' unfeeling for his own.
Yet ah ! why should they know their fate ?
Since sorrow never comes too late,
And happiness too swiftly flies.
Thought would destroy their paradise.
No more ; where ignorance is bliss,
'Tis folly to be wise.   100

H Y M N

TO

ADVERSITY.

———Ζῆνα
Τὸν φρονεῖν βροτοὺς ὁδώ-
σαντα, τῷ πάθει μάθαν
Θέντα κυρίως ἔχειν.

ÆSCHYLUS, in Agamemnone.

[There is one MS. in the Commonplace Book, dated 'at Stoke, Aug. 1742'. This has two variants. There is another MS. in Gray's letter to Walpole of 8 September, 1751 (Letter 161).]

H Y M N

TO

A D V E R S I T Y.

Daughter of Jove, relentless Power,
Thou Tamer of the human breast,
Whose iron scourge and tort'ring hour,
The Bad affright, afflict the Best !
Bound in thy adamantine chain
The Proud are taught to taste of pain,
And purple Tyrants vainly groan
With pangs unfelt before, unpitied and alone.

When first thy Sire to send on earth
Virtue, his darling Child, design'd,
To thee he gave the heav'nly Birth,
And bad to form her infant mind.

to

Stern rugged Nurse ! thy rigid lore
With patience many a year she bore :
What sorrow was, thou bad'st her know,
And from her own she learn'd to melt at others' woe.

Scared at thy frown terrific, fly
Self-pleasing Folly's idle brood,
Wild Laughter, Noise, and thoughtless Joy,
And leave us leisure to be good.   20
Light they disperse, and with them go
The summer Friend, the flatt'ring Foe ;
By vain Prosperity received,
To her they vow their truth, and are again believed.

Wisdom in sable garb array'd
Immers'd in rapt'rous thought profound,
And Melancholy, silent maid
With leaden eye, that loves the ground,
Still on thy solemn steps attend :
Warm Charity, the gen'ral Friend,   30
With Justice to herself severe,
And Pity, dropping soft the sadly-pleasing tear.

Oh, gently on thy Suppliant's head,
Dread Goddess, lay thy chast'ning hand !
Not in thy Gorgon terrors clad,
Nor circled with the vengeful Band

(As by the Impious thou art seen)
With thund'ring voice, and threat'ning mien,
With screaming Horror's funeral cry,
Despair, and fell Disease, and ghastly Poverty.   40

Thy form benign, oh Goddess, wear,
Thy milder influence impart,
Thy philosophic Train be there
To soften, not to wound my heart.
The gen'rous spark extinct revive,
Teach me to love and to forgive,
Exact my own defects to scan,
What others are, to feel, and know myself a Man.

THE

PROGRESS of POESY.

A PINDARIC ODE.

Φωνᾶντα συνετοῖσιν· ἐς
Δὲ τὸ πᾶν ἑρμηνέων χατίζει.

PINDAR, Olymp. II.

ADVERTISEMENT.

When the Author first published this and the following
Ode, he was advised, even by his Friends, to subjoin
some few explanatory Notes; but had too much
respect for the understanding of his Readers to take
that liberty.

[The Ode was sent to Wharton in a letter dated December 26,
1754. Lines 1 to 24 were sent to Bedingfield on December 29,
1756. There is another copy in Gray's handwriting among the
Pembroke MSS., at the foot of which is noted ' finish'd in 1754,
printed together with *The Bard, An Ode*, Aug: 8, 1757 '. The
two poems (with the title of *Odes*) formed the first volume
issued from Horace Walpole's Press at Strawberry Hill. The
notes and advertisement were added in the edition of 1768.]

THE

PROGRESS of POESY.

A PINDARIC ODE.

I. 1.

* AWAKE, Æolian lyre, awake,

And give to rapture all thy trembling strings.

From Helicon's harmonious springs

A thousand rills their mazy progress take :

The laughing flowers, that round them blow,

Drink life and fragrance as they flow.

---

*   Awake, my glory : awake, lute and harp.

David's Psalms.

Pindar styles his own poetry with its musical accompanyments,
Αἰοληῒς μολπή, Αἰολίδες χορδαί, Αἰολίδων πνοαὶ αὐλῶν, Æolian song,
Æolian strings, the breath of the Æolian flute.

The subject and simile, as usual with Pindar, are united. The
various sources of poetry, which gives life and lustre to all it touches,
are here described ; its quiet majestic progress enriching every
subject (otherwise dry and barren) with a pomp of diction and
luxuriant harmony of numbers ; and its more rapid and irresistible
course, when swoln and hurried away by the conflict of tumultuous
passions.

Now the rich stream of music winds along

Deep, majestic, smooth, and strong,

Thro' verdant vales, and Ceres' golden reign :

Now rowling down the steep amain,   10

Headlong, impetuous, see it pour :

The rocks, and nodding groves rebellow to the roar.

I. 2.

 * Oh ! Sovereign of the willing soul,

Parent of sweet and solemn-breathing airs,

Enchanting shell ! the sullen Cares,

And frantic Passions hear thy soft controul.

On Thracia's hills the Lord of War,

Has curb'd the fury of his car,

And drop'd his thirsty lance at thy command.

† Perching on the scept'red hand   20

Of Jove, thy magic lulls the feather'd king

With ruffled plumes, and flagging wing :

Quench'd in dark clouds of slumber lie

The terror of his beak, and light'nings of his eye.

 * Power of harmony to calm the turbulent sallies of the soul.
The thoughts are borrowed from the first Pythian of Pindar.
 † This is a weak imitation of some incomparable lines in the same
Ode.

I. 3.

* Thee the voice, the dance, obey,
Temper'd to thy warbled lay.
O'er Idalia's velvet-green
The rosy-crowned Loves are seen
On Cytherea's day
With antic Sports, and blue-eyed Pleasures,   30
Frisking light in frolic measures ;
Now pursuing, now retreating,
Now in circling troops they meet :
To brisk notes in cadence beating
† Glance their many-twinkling feet.
Slow melting strains their Queen's approach declare :
Where'er she turns the Graces homage pay.
With arms sublime, that float upon the air,
In gliding state she wins her easy way :
O'er her warm cheek, and rising bosom, move   40
‡ The bloom of young Desire, and purple light of Love.

* Power of harmony to produce all the graces of motion in the body.
† Μαρμαρυγὰς θηεῖτο ποδῶν, θαύμαζε δὲ θυμῷ.   HOMER. Od. Θ.
‡ Λάμπει δ' ἐπὶ πορφυρέῃσι
   Παρείῃσι φῶς ἔρωτος.   PHRYNICHUS, apud Athenæum.

II.   1.

* Man's feeble race what Ills await,

Labour, and Penury, the racks of Pain,

Disease, and Sorrow's weeping train,

And Death, sad refuge from the storms of Fate!

The fond complaint, my Song, disprove,

And justify the laws of Jove.

Say, has he giv'n in vain the heav'nly Muse?

Night, and all her sickly dews,

Her Spectres wan, and Birds of boding cry,   50

He gives to range the dreary sky:

† Till down the eastern cliffs afar

Hyperion's march they spy, and glitt'ring shafts of war.

II.   2

‡ In climes beyond the solar § road,

Where shaggy forms o'er ice-built mountains roam,

---

* To compensate the real and imaginary ills of life, the Muse was given to Mankind by the same Providence that sends the Day by its chearful presence to dispel the gloom and terrors of the Night.

†   Or seen the Morning's well-appointed Star
          Come marching up the eastern hills afar.   *Cowley.*

‡ Extensive influence of poetic Genius over the remotest and most uncivilized nations : its connection with liberty, and the virtues that naturally attend on it. [See the Erse, Norwegian, and Welch Fragments, the Lapland and American songs.]

§ " Extra anni solisque vias——"   *Virgil.*

" Tutta lontana dai camin del sole." *Petrarch, Canzon* 2.

The Muse has broke the twilight-gloom

To chear the shiv'ring Native's dull abode.

And oft, beneath the od'rous shade

Of Chili's boundless forests laid,

She deigns to hear the savage Youth repeat   60

In loose numbers wildly sweet

Their feather-cinctured Chiefs, and dusky Loves.

Her track, where'er the Goddess roves,

Glory pursue, and generous Shame,

Th' unconquerable Mind, and Freedom's holy flame.

II. 3.

* Woods, that wave o'er Delphi's steep,

Isles, that crown th' Egæan deep,

Fields, that cool Ilissus laves,

Or where Mæander's amber waves

In lingering Lab'rinths creep,   70

How do your tuneful Echoes languish,

Mute, but to the voice of Anguish?

* Progress of Poetry from Greece to Italy, and from Italy to England. Chaucer was not unacquainted with the writings of Dante or of Petrarch. The Earl of Surrey and Sir Tho. Wyatt had travelled in Italy, and formed their taste there; Spenser imitated the Italian writers; Milton improved on them: but this School expired soon after the Restoration, and a new one arose on the French model, which has subsisted ever since.

[l. 71 Echoes *misprinted* Echo's *in Poems* (1768).]

Where each old poetic Mountain
Inspiration breath'd around :
Ev'ry shade and hallow'd Fountain
Murmur'd deep a solemn sound :
Till the sad Nine in Greece's evil hour
Left their Parnassus for the Latian plains.
Alike they scorn the pomp of tyrant-Power,
And coward Vice, that revels in her chains.   80
When Latium had her lofty spirit lost,
They sought, oh Albion ! next thy sea-encircled coast.

III. 1.

   Far from the sun and summer-gale,
In thy green lap was Nature's * Darling laid,
What time, where lucid Avon stray'd,
To Him the mighty Mother did unveil
Her aweful face : The dauntless Child
Stretch'd forth his little arms, and smiled.
This pencil take (she said) whose colours clear
Richly paint the vernal year :   90
Thine too these golden keys, immortal Boy !
This can unlock the gates of Joy ;
Of Horrour that, and thrilling Fears,
Or ope the sacred source of sympathetic Tears.

* Shakespear.

HUGH STEPHENS LIBRARY
STEPHENS COLLEGE
COLUMBIA, MISSOURI

III. 2.

Nor second He *, that rode sublime

Upon the seraph-wings of Extasy,

The secrets of th' Abyss to spy.

† He pass'd the flaming bounds of Place and Time :

‡ The living Throne, the saphire-blaze,

Where Angels tremble, while they gaze,   100

He saw ; but blasted with excess of light,

§ Closed his eyes in endless night.

Behold, where Dryden's less presumptuous car,

Wide o'er the fields of Glory bear

‖ Two Coursers of ethereal race,

¶ With necks in thunder cloath'd, and long-resounding
    pace.

III. 3.

Hark, his hands the lyre explore !

Bright-eyed Fancy hovering o'er

* Milton.
† " ——flammantia mœnia mundi."   *Lucretius.*
‡ For the spirit of the living creature was in the wheels—And
above the firmament, that was over their heads, was the likeness
of a throne, as the appearance of a saphire-stone.—This was the
appearance of the glory of the Lord.   *Ezekiel* i. 20, 26, 28.
§ Ὀφθαλμῶν μὲν ἄμερσε· δίδου δ' ἡδεῖαν ἀοιδήν.   Homer. Od.
‖ Meant to express the stately march and sounding energy of
Dryden's rhimes.
¶ Hast thou cloathed his neck with thunder ?   *Job.*

103566

Scatters from her pictur'd urn

* Thoughts, that breath, and words, that burn.   110

† But ah ! 'tis heard no more——

Oh ! Lyre divine, what daring Spirit

Wakes thee now ? Tho' he inherit

Nor the pride, nor ample pinion,

‡ That the Theban Eagle bear

Sailing with supreme dominion

Thro' the azure deep of air :

Yet oft before his infant eyes would run

Such forms, as glitter in the Muse's ray

With orient hues, unborrow'd of the Sun :   120

Yet shall he mount, and keep his distant way

Beyond the limits of a vulgar fate,

Beneath the Good how far—but far above the Great.

---

* Words, that weep, and tears, that speak.   *Cowley.*

† We have had in our language no other odes of the sublime kind, than that of Dryden on St. Cecilia's day : for Cowley (who had his merit) yet wanted judgment, style, and harmony, for such a task. That of Pope is not worthy of so great a man. Mr. Mason indeed of late days has touched the true chords, and with a masterly hand, in some of his Choruses,—above all in the last of Caractacus,

Hark ! heard ye not yon footstep dread ? *&c.*

‡ Διὸς πρὸς ὄρνιχα θεῖον. Olymp. 2. Pindar compares himself to that bird, and his enemies to ravens that croak and clamour in vain below, while it pursues its flight, regardless of their noise.

THE

BARD.

A PINDARIC ODE,

ADVERTISEMENT.

The following Ode is founded on a Tradition current in Wales, that EDWARD THE FIRST, when he compleated the conquest of that country, ordered all the Bards, that fell into his hands, to be put to death.

[It was begun in December 1754 : the first part was sent to Wharton before August 6, 1755, and a further portion was sent to Stonhewer and passed on to Wharton towards the end of the month. Gray then laid it aside until May 1757, when he was freshly inspired by hearing Parry, a Welsh harper, and finished it. It was published in August of that year (see preliminary note to *Progress of Poesy*). Parts of the poem, before it was finished, were sent to Bedingfield, Mason, and Wharton (see notes).]

THE

B A R D.

A PINDARIC ODE.

I. 1.

' Ruin seize thee, ruthless King !

' Confusion on thy banners wait,

' Tho' fann'd by Conquest's crimson wing

' * They mock the air with idle state.

' Helm, nor † Hauberk's twisted mail,

' Nor even thy virtues, Tyrant, shall avail

' To save thy secret soul from nightly fears,

' From Cambria's curse, from Cambria's tears ! '

Such were the sounds, that o'er the ‡ crested pride

---

   *   Mocking the air with colours idly spread.
                                   Shakespear's King John.
   † The Hauberk was a texture of steel ringlets, or rings interwoven, forming a coat of mail, that sate close to the body, and adapted itself to every motion.
   ‡ ——The crested adder's pride.   *Dryden's Indian Queen.*

Of the first Edward scatter'd wild dismay,   10

As down the steep of * Snowdon's shaggy side

He wound with toilsome march his long array.

Stout † Glo'ster stood aghast in speechless trance :

To arms! cried ‡Mortimer, and couch'd his quiv'ring lance.

I. 2.

On a rock, whose haughty brow

Frowns o'er old Conway's foaming flood,

Robed in the sable garb of woe,

With haggard eyes the Poet stood ;

(§ Loose his beard, and hoary hair

‖ Stream'd, like a meteor, to the troubled air)   20

* *Snowdon* was a name given by the Saxons to that mountainous tract, which the Welch themselves call *Craigian-eryri* : it included all the highlands of Caernarvonshire and Merionethshire, as far east as the river Conway. R. Hygden speaking of the castle of Conway built by King Edward the first, says, ' Ad ortum amnis Conway ' ad clivum montis Erery ; ' and Matthew of Westminster, (ad ann. 1283,) ' Apud Aberconway ad pedes montis Snowdoniæ fecit erigi ' castrum forte.'

† Gilbert de Clare, surnamed the Red, Earl of Gloucester and Hertford, son-in-law to King Edward.

‡ Edmond de Mortimer, Lord of Wigmore.

They both were *Lords-Marchers*, whose lands lay on the borders of Wales, and probably accompanied the King in this expedition.

§ The image was taken from a well-known picture of Raphaël, representing the Supreme Being in the vision of Ezekiel : there are two of these paintings (both believed original), one at Florence, the other at Paris.

‖   Shone, like a meteor, streaming to the wind.

Milton's Paradise Lost.

And with a Master's hand, and Prophet's fire,

Struck the deep sorrows of his lyre.

' Hark, how each giant-oak, and desert cave,

' Sighs to the torrent's aweful voice beneath !

' O'er thee, oh King ! their hundred arms they wave,

' Revenge on thee in hoarser murmurs breath ;

' Vocal no more, since Cambria's fatal day,

' To high-born Hoel's harp, or soft Llewellyn's lay.

I. 3.

  ' Cold is Cadwallo's tongue,

' That hush'd the stormy main :   3c

' Brave Urien sleeps upon his craggy bed :

' Mountains, ye mourn in vain

' Modred, whose magic song

' Made huge Plinlimmon bow his cloud-top'd head.

' * On dreary Arvon's shore they lie,

' Smear'd with gore, and ghastly pale :

' Far, far aloof th' affrighted ravens fail ;

' The famish'd † Eagle screams, and passes by.

---

  * The shores of Caernarvonshire opposite to the isle of Anglesey.

  † Cambden and others observe, that eagles used annually to build
their aerie among the rocks of Snowdon, which from thence (as
some think) were named by the Welch *Craigian-eryri*, or the crags
of the eagles. At this day (I am told) the highest point of Snowdon
is called *the eagle's nest*. That bird is certainly no stranger to this

' Dear lost companions of my tuneful art,

' * Dear, as the light that visits these sad eyes,   40

' * Dear, as the ruddy drops that warm my heart,

' Ye died amidst your dying country's cries—

' No more I weep.   They do not sleep.

' On yonder cliffs, a griesly band,

' I see them sit, they linger yet,

' Avengers of their native land :

' With me in dreadful harmony † they join,

' And † weave with bloody hands the tissue of thy line.'

II.   1.

" Weave the warp, and weave the woof,

" The winding-sheet of Edward's race.   50

" Give ample room, and verge enough

" The characters of hell to trace.

" Mark the year, and mark the night,

" ‡ When Severn shall re-eccho with affright

" The shrieks of death, thro' Berkley's roofs that ring,

" Shrieks of an agonizing King !

island, as the Scots, and the people of Cumberland, Westmoreland, &c. can testify : it even has built its nest in the Peak of Derbyshire. [See Willoughby's Ornithol. published by Ray.]

   * As dear to me as are the ruddy drops,
     That visit my sad heart———   *Shakesp. Jul. Cæsar.*
   † See the Norwegian Ode, that follows.
   ‡ Edward the Second, cruelly butchered in Berkley-Castle.

" * She-Wolf of France, with unrelenting fangs,

" That tear'st the bowels of thy mangled Mate,

" † From thee be born, who o'er thy country hangs

" The scourge of Heav'n. What Terrors round him

    wait !   60

" Amazement in his van, with Flight combined,

" And sorrow's faded form, and solitude behind.

II. 2.

 " Mighty Victor, mighty Lord,

" ‡ Low on his funeral couch he lies !

" No pitying heart, no eye, afford

" A tear to grace his obsequies.

" Is the sable § Warriour fled ?

" Thy son is gone.   He rests among the Dead.

" The Swarm, that in thy noon-tide beam were born ?

" Gone to salute the rising Morn.   70

" Fair ‖ laughs the Morn, and soft the Zephyr blows,

" While proudly riding o'er the azure realm

---

* Isabel of France, Edward the Second's adulterous Queen.

† Triumphs of Edward the Third in France.

‡ Death of that King, abandoned by his Children, and even robbed in his last moments by his Courtiers and his Mistress.

§ Edward, the Black Prince, dead some time before his Father.

‖ Magnificence of Richard the Second's reign. See Froissard, and other contemporary Writers.

" In gallant trim the gilded Vessel goes ;

" Youth on the prow, and Pleasure at the helm ;

" Regardless of the sweeping Whirlwind's sway,

" That, hush'd in grim repose, expects his evening-prey.

II. 3.

" * Fill high the sparkling bowl,

" The rich repast prepare,

" Reft of a crown, he yet may share the feast :

" Close by the regal chair   80

" Fell Thirst and Famine scowl

" A baleful smile upon their baffled Guest.

" Heard ye the din of † battle bray,

" Lance to lance, and horse to horse ?

" Long Years of havock urge their destined course,

" And thro' the kindred squadrons mow their way.

" Ye Towers of Julius ‡, London's lasting shame,

" With many a foul and midnight murther fed,

* Richard the Second, (as we are told by Archbishop Scroop and the confederate Lords in their manifesto, by Thomas of Walsingham, and all the older Writers,) was starved to death. The story of his assassination by Sir Piers of Exon, is of much later date.

† Ruinous civil wars of York and Lancaster.

‡ Henry the Sixth, George Duke of Clarence, Edward the Fifth, Richard Duke of York, &c. believed to be murthered secretly in the Tower of London. The oldest part of that structure is vulgarly attributed to Julius Cæsar.

" Revere his * Consort's faith, his Father's † fame,

" And spare the meek ‡ Usurper's holy head.   90

" Above, below, the § rose of snow,

" Twined with her blushing foe, we spread :

" The bristled ‖ Boar in infant-gore

" Wallows beneath the thorny shade.

" Now, Brothers, bending o'er th' accursed loom

" Stamp we our vengeance deep, and ratify his doom.

III. 1.

" Edward, lo ! to sudden fate

" (Weave we the woof.   The thread is spun)

" ¶ Half of thy heart we consecrate.

" (The web is wove.   The work is done.) "   100

' Stay, oh stay ! nor thus forlorn

' Leave me unbless'd, unpitied, here to mourn :

* Margaret of Anjou, a woman of heroic spirit, who struggled
hard to save her Husband and her Crown.

† Henry the Fifth.

‡ Henry the Sixth very near being canonized. The line of Lancaster had no right of inheritance to the Crown.

§ The white and red roses, devices of York and Lancaster.

‖ The silver Boar was the badge of Richard the Third ; whence
he was usually known in his own time by the name of *the Boar.*

¶ Eleanor of Castile died a few years after the conquest of Wales.
The heroic proof she gave of her affection for her Lord is well known.
The monuments of his regret, and sorrow for the loss of her, are
still to be seen at Northampton, Geddington, Waltham, and other
places.

' In yon bright track, that fires the western skies,

' They melt, they vanish from my eyes.

' But oh ! what solemn scenes on Snowdon's height

' Descending slow their glitt'ring skirts unroll ?

' Visions of glory, spare my aching sight,

' Ye unborn Ages, crowd not on my soul !

' No more our long-lost * Arthur we bewail.   109

' All-hail, † ye genuine Kings, Britannia's Issue, hail !

III. 2.

  ' Girt with many a Baron bold

' Sublime their starry fronts they rear ;

' And gorgeous Dames, and Statesmen old

' In bearded majesty, appear.

' In the midst a Form divine !

' Her eye proclaims her of the Briton-Line ;

' Her lyon-port ‡, her awe-commanding face,

' Attemper'd sweet to virgin-grace.

* It was the common belief of the Welch nation, that King Arthur was still alive in Fairy-Land, and should return again to reign over Britain.

† Both Merlin and Taliessin had prophesied, that the Welch should regain their sovereignty over this island ; which seemed to be accomplished in the House of Tudor.

‡ Speed relating an audience given by Queen Elizabeth to Paul Dzialinski, Ambassadour of Poland, says, ' And thus she, lion-like ' rising, daunted the malapert Orator no less with her stately port ' and majestical deporture, than with the tartnesse of her princelie ' checkes.'

' What strings symphonious tremble in the air,

' What strains of vocal transport round her play !   120

' Hear from the grave, great Taliessin *, hear ;

' They breathe a soul to animate thy clay.

' Bright Rapture calls, and soaring, as she sings,

' Waves in the eye of Heav'n her many-colour'd wings.

III. 3.

  ' The verse adorn again

' † Fierce War, and faithful Love,

' And Truth severe, by fairy Fiction drest.

' In ‡ buskin'd measures move

' Pale Grief, and pleasing Pain,

' With Horrour, Tyrant of the throbbing breast.   130

' A § Voice, as of the Cherub-Choir,

' Gales from blooming Eden bear ;

' ‖ And distant warblings lessen on my ear,

' That lost in long futurity expire.

* Taliessin, Chief of the Bards, flourished in the VIth Century. His works are still preserved, and his memory held in high veneration among his Countrymen.

† Fierce wars and faithful loves shall moralize my song.
Spenser's Proëme to the Fairy Queen.

‡ Shakespear.
§ Milton.
‖ The succession of Poets after Milton's time.

' Fond impious Man, think'st thou, yon sanguine cloud,

' Rais'd by thy breath, has quench'd the Orb of day ?

' To-morrow he repairs the golden flood,

' And warms the nations with redoubled ray.

' Enough for me : With joy I see

' The different doom our Fates assign.   140

' Be thine Despair, and scept'red Care,

' To triumph, and to die, are mine.'

He spoke, and headlong from the mountain's height

Deep in the roaring tide he plung'd to endless night.

THE

FATAL SISTERS.

AN ODE,

(From the NORSE-TONGUE,)

IN THE

ORCADES of THORMODUS TORFÆUS;
HAFNIÆ, 1697, Folio: and also in
BARTHOLINUS.

VITT ER ORPIT FYRIR VALFALLI, &C.

P

[The MS. at Pembroke bears the date 1761 and is entitled 'The Song of the Valkyries'. There is also a transcript in Wharton's handwriting with the title 'The Song of the Weird Sisters, translated from the Norwegian written about 1029'. The ode is a paraphrase of an Icelandic poem of the eleventh century entitled *Darraðar Lióð*, or 'Lay of Darts.' It refers to the battle of Clontarf, which was fought on Good Friday 1014. It was, like the two following odes, first published in the edition of 1768 'to make up', as he says in a letter to James Beattie, February 1, 1768, 'for the omission of that *Long Story*'.]

ADVERTISEMENT.

The Author once had thoughts (in concert with a Friend)
of giving *the History of English Poetry* : In the Introduction to it he meant to have produced some specimens
of the Style that reigned in ancient times among the
neighbouring nations, or those who had subdued the
greater part of this Island, and were our Progenitors :
the following three Imitations made a part of them.
He has long since drop'd his design, especially after
he had heard, that it was already in the hands of
a Person well qualified to do it justice, both by his
taste, and his researches into antiquity.

PREFACE.

In the Eleventh Century *Sigurd*, Earl of the Orkney-Islands, went with a fleet of ships and a considerable body of troops into Ireland, to the assistance of *Sictryg with the silken beard*, who was then making war on his father-in-law *Brian*, King of Dublin : the Earl and all his forces were cut to pieces, and *Sictryg* was in danger of a total defeat ; but the enemy had a greater loss by the death of *Brian*, their King, who fell in the action. On Christmas-day, (the day of the battle,) a Native of *Caithness* in Scotland saw at a distance a number of persons on horseback riding full speed towards a hill, and seeming to enter into it. Curiosity led him to follow them, till looking through an opening in the rocks he saw twelve gigantic figures resembling women : they were all employed about a loom ; and as they wove, they sung the following dreadful Song ; which when they had finished, they tore the web into twelve pieces, and (each taking her portion) galloped Six to the North and as many to the South.

THE

FATAL SISTERS.

AN ODE.

Now the storm begins to lower,
(Haste, the loom of Hell prepare,)
* Iron-sleet of arrowy shower
† Hurtles in the darken'd air.

Glitt'ring lances are the loom,
Where the dusky warp we strain,
Weaving many a Soldier's doom,
Orkney's woe, and *Randver*'s bane.

Note—The *Valkyriur* were female Divinities, Servants of *Odin* (or *Woden*) in the Gothic mythology. Their name signifies *Chusers of the slain*. They were mounted on swift horses, with drawn swords in their hands; and in the throng of battle selected such as were destined to slaughter, and conducted them to *Valhalla*, the hall of *Odin*, or paradise of the Brave; where they attended the banquet, and served the departed Heroes with horns of mead and ale.

  * How quick they wheel'd; and flying, behind them shot
    Sharp sleet of arrowy shower—— *Milton's Par. Regained.*
  † The noise of battle hurtled in the air.   *Shakesp. Jul. Cæsar.*

    [In line 5 of *Note* Dodsley misprinted 'Valkalla'.]

See the griesly texture grow,
('Tis of human entrails made,)   10
And the weights, that play below,
Each a gasping Warriour's head.

Shafts for shuttles, dipt in gore,
Shoot the trembling cords along.
Sword, that once a Monarch bore,
Keep the tissue close and strong.

Mista black, terrific Maid,
Sangrida, and *Hilda* see,
Join the wayward work to aid :
'Tis the woof of victory.   20

Ere the ruddy sun be set,
Pikes must shiver, javelins sing,
Blade with clattering buckler meet,
Hauberk crash, and helmet ring.

(Weave the crimson web of war)
Let us go, and let us fly,
Where our Friends the conflict share,
Where they triumph, where they die.

As the paths of fate we tread,
Wading thro' th' ensanguin'd field :   30
Gondula, and *Geira,* spread
O'er the youthful King your shield.

We the reins to slaughter give,
Ours to kill, and ours to spare :
Spite of danger he shall live.
(Weave the crimson web of war.)

They, whom once the desart-beach
Pent within its bleak domain,
Soon their ample sway shall stretch
O'er the plenty of the plain.   40

Low the dauntless Earl is laid,
Gor'd with many a gaping wound :
Fate demands a nobler head ;
Soon a King shall bite the ground.

Long his loss shall Eirin weep,
Ne'er again his likeness see ;
Long her strains in sorrow steep,
Strains of Immortality !

Horror covers all the heath,
Clouds of carnage blot the sun.   50
Sisters, weave the web of death ;
Sisters, cease, the work is done.

Hail the task, and hail the hands !
Songs of joy and triumph sing !
Joy to the victorious bands ;
Triumph to the younger King.

Mortal, thou that hear'st the tale,
Learn the tenour of our song.
Scotland, thro' each winding vale
Far and wide the notes prolong.   60

Sisters, hence with spurs of speed :
Each her thundering faulchion wield ;
Each bestride her sable steed.
Hurry, hurry to the field.

THE

DESCENT of ODIN.

AN ODE,

(From the Norse-Tongue,)

IN

BARTHOLINUS, de causis contemnendæ mortis ;
HAFNIÆ, 1689, Quarto.

UPREIS ODINN ALLDA GAUTR, &c.

[Written at Cambridge 1761 and first published in the edition of 1768. There is a MS. at Pembroke and a transcript in Wharton's handwriting among the Egerton MSS. in the British Museum (No. 2400) under the title 'The Vegtams Kwitha from Bartholinus'. It is taken from the Icelandic poem *Vegtams Kviða* or *Baldrs draumer*.]

THE

DESCENT of ODIN.

AN ODE.

Uprose the King of Men with speed,
And saddled strait his coal-black steed;
Down the yawning steep he rode,
That leads to * Hela's drear abode.
Him the Dog of Darkness spied,
His shaggy throat he open'd wide,
While from his jaws, with carnage fill'd,
Foam and human gore distill'd:
Hoarse he bays with hideous din,
Eyes that glow, and fangs, that grin;   10
And long pursues, with fruitless yell,
The Father of the powerful spell.

* *Niflheimr*, the hell of the Gothic nations, consisted of nine worlds, to which were devoted all such as died of sickness, old-age, or by any other means than in battle: Over it presided Hela, the Goddess of Death.

Onward still his way he takes,
(The groaning earth beneath him shakes,)
Till full before his fearless eyes
The portals nine of hell arise.

  Right against the eastern gate,
By the moss-grown pile he sate;
Where long of yore to sleep was laid
The dust of the prophetic Maid.   20
Facing to the northern clime,
Thrice he traced the runic rhyme;
Thrice pronounc'd, in accents dread,
The thrilling verse that wakes the Dead;
Till from out the hollow ground
Slowly breath'd a sullen sound.

  PR.   What call unknown, what charms presume
To break the quiet of the tomb?
Who thus afflicts my troubled sprite,
And drags me from the realms of night?   30
Long on these mould'ring bones have beat
The winter's snow, the summer's heat,
The drenching dews, and driving rain!
Let me, let me sleep again.
Who is he, with voice unblest,
That calls me from the bed of rest?

O.   A Traveller, to thee unknown,
Is he that calls, a Warriour's Son.
Thou the deeds of light shalt know ;
Tell me what is done below,   40
For whom yon glitt'ring board is spread,
Drest for whom yon golden bed.

Pr.   Mantling in the goblet see
The pure bev'rage of the bee,
O'er it hangs the shield of gold ;
'Tis the drink of *Balder* bold :
Balder's head to death is giv'n.
Pain can reach the Sons of Heav'n !
Unwilling I my lips unclose :
Leave me, leave me to repose.   50

O.   Once again my call obey.
Prophetess, arise, and say,
What dangers *Odin*'s Child await,
Who the Author of his fate.

Pr.   In *Hoder*'s hand the Heroe's doom :
His Brother sends him to the tomb.
Now my weary lips I close :
Leave me, leave me to repose.

O.   Prophetess, my spell obey,
Once again arise, and say,   60
Who th' Avenger of his guilt,
By whom shall *Hoder*'s blood be spilt.

PR.   In the caverns of the west,
By *Odin*'s fierce embrace comprest,
A wond'rous Boy shall *Rinda* bear,
Who ne'er shall comb his raven-hair,
Nor wash his visage in the stream,
Nor see the sun's departing beam ;
Till he on *Hoder's* corse shall smile
Flaming on the fun'ral pile.   70
Now my weary lips I close :
Leave me, leave me to repose.

O.   Yet a while my call obey.
Prophetess, awake, and say,
What Virgins these, in speechless woe,
That bend to earth their solemn brow,
That their flaxen tresses tear,
And snowy veils, that float in air.
Tell me whence their sorrows rose :
Then I leave thee to repose.   80

Pr. Ha ! no Traveller art thou,
King of Men, I know thee now,
Mightiest of a mighty line——

O. No boding Maid of skill divine
Art thou, nor Prophetess of good ;
But Mother of the giant-brood !

Pr. Hie thee hence, and boast at home,
That never shall Enquirer come
To break my iron-sleep again ;
Till * *Lok* has burst his tenfold chain.   90
Never, till substantial Night
Has reassum'd her ancient right ;
Till wrap'd in flames, in ruin hurl'd,
Sinks the fabric of the world.

* *Lok* is the evil Being, who continues in chains till the *Twilight of the Gods* approaches, when he shall break his bonds ; the human race, the stars, and sun, shall disappear ; the earth sink in the seas, and fire consume the skies : even Odin himself and his kindred-deities shall perish. For a farther explanation of this mythology, see Mallet's Introduction to the History of Denmark, 1755, Quarto.

THE

TRIUMPHS of OWEN.

A FRAGMENT.

FROM

Mr. EVANS's Specimens of the Welch Poetry;
LONDON, 1764, Quarto.

ADVERTISEMENT.

OWEN succeeded his Father GRIFFIN in the Principality of North-Wales, A. D. 1120. This battle was fought near forty Years afterwards.

[The ode, written probably in 1761 (see *Correspondence*, Appendix M), was first published with the advertisement and notes in the edition of 1768. It is preserved in Gray's handwriting among the Pembroke MSS.]

THE

TRIUMPHS of OWEN.

A FRAGMENT.

Owen's praise demands my song,
Owen swift, and Owen strong;
Fairest flower of Roderic's stem,
* Gwyneth's shield, and Britain's gem.
He nor heaps his brooded stores,
Nor on all profusely pours;
Lord of every regal art,
Liberal hand, and open heart.

Big with hosts of mighty name,
Squadrons three against him came;   10

* North-Wales.

This the force of Eirin hiding,
Side by side as proudly riding,
On her shadow long and gay
* Lochlin plows the watry way ;
There the Norman sails afar
Catch the winds, and join the war :
Black and huge along they sweep,
Burthens of the angry deep.

Dauntless on his native sands
† The Dragon-Son of Mona stands ;   20
In glitt'ring arms and glory drest,
High he rears his ruby crest.
There the thund'ring strokes begin,
There the press, and there the din ;
Talymalfra's rocky shore
Echoing to the battle's roar.
Where his glowing eye-balls turn,
Thousand Banners round him burn.
Where he points his purple spear,
Hasty, hasty Rout is there,   30
Marking with indignant eye
Fear to stop, and shame to fly.

* Denmark.
† The red Dragon is the device of Cadwallader, which all his
descendents bore on their banners.

There Confusion, Terror's child,
Conflict fierce, and Ruin wild,
Agony, that pants for breath,
Despair and honourable Death.

*   *   *

ELEGY

WRITTEN IN A

COUNTRY CHURCH-YARD.

[According to Mason, the *Elegy* was begun in August 1742; but we can only say for certain that Gray wrote the main portion of the poem between 1746 and 1750. It was finished by June 12, 1750. On February 10, 1751, the editors of the *Magazine of Magazines* asked for permission to print it. Gray refused and at once wrote to Horace Walpole asking him to publish it anonymously. On February 15 it appeared as a quarto pamphlet under the title *An Elegy wrote in a Country Church Yard*, together with the following preface by Walpole: 'The following *Poem* came into my hands by Accident, if the general Approbation with which this little Piece has been spread, may be call'd by so slight a term as Accident. It is this Approbation which makes it unnecessary for me to make any Apology but to the Author: As he cannot but feel some Satisfaction in having pleas'd so many Readers already, I flatter myself he will forgive my communicating that Pleasure to many more. The Editor.'

The text here printed is taken from the edition of 1768. Three copies of the *Elegy* in Gray's handwriting are still preserved. The MS. formerly in the possession of Sir W. Fraser and now at Eton College contains probably the original draft. This differs considerably from the form in which the poem was published, and for this reason it is printed below (Appendix I). A second copy was sent to Wharton and is among the Egerton MSS. at the British Museum (No. 2400), and a third is at Pembroke College. The variations in these two manuscripts are given in the notes. The following bibliographical note is appended to the Pembroke MS. in Gray's writing: '1750. publish'd in Feb:^{ry} 1751. by Dodsley; and went through four [*five* cancelled] editions;

in two months; and afterwards a fifth, 6th, 7th, & 8th 9th & 10th & 11th. printed also in 1753 with Mr Bentley's Designs, of wch there is a 2^d Edition & again by Dodsley in his Miscellany Vol. 4th & in a Scotch Collection call'd the *Union*. translated into Latin by Ch^r Anstey Esq. & the Rev. Mr Roberts, & publish'd in 1762, & again in the same year by Rob: Lloyd M: A:'. For the history of its publication and an account of the different editions, etc., see *An Elegy . . . by Thomas Gray*, ed. F. G. Stokes, Oxford, 1929.]

Far from the madding Croud's ignoble Strife,
Their sober Wishes never learn'd to stray;
Along the cool sequester'd Vale of Life
They kept the noiseless Tenour of their Way.

Yet ev'n these Bones from Insult to protect
Some frail Memorial still erected nigh,
With uncouth Rhimes, & shapeless Sculpture deck'd,
Implores the passing Tribute of a sigh.   80.

Their Name, their Years, spelt by th' unletter'd Muse
The Place of Fame & Epitaph supply;
And many a holy Text around she strews,
That teach the rustic Moralist to die.

For who to dumb Forgetfullness a Prey,
This pleasing anxious Being e'er resign'd,
Left the warm Precincts of the chearful Day,
Nor cast one longing ling'ring Look behind?   100.

On some fond Breast the parting Soul relies,
Some pious Drops the closing Eye requires;
Even from the Tomb the Voice of Nature cries,   Ev'n   live
And in our Ashes glow their wonted Fires.

For Thee, who mindful of th' unhonour'd Dead
Dost in these Lines their artless Tale relate:
If chance, by lonely Contemplation led,
Some kindred Spirit shall enquire thy Fate;

Haply some hoary-headed Swain may say,
 "Oft have we seen him at the Peep of Dawn
 "Brushing with hasty Steps the Dews away   110.
 "To meet the Sun upon the upland Lawn.

 "There, at the Foot of yonder nodding Beech,
 "That wreaths its old fantastic Roots so high,
 "His listless Length at Noontide would he stretch,
 "And pore upon the Brook, that babbles by.

 "Hard by yon Wood, now smiling as in Scorn,
 "Muttering his wayward Fancies, would he rove;
 "Now drooping, woeful-wan, like one forlorn,
 "Or crazed with Care, or cross'd in hopeless Love.

 "One Morn I miss'd him from the custom'd Hill,   120.
 "Along the Heath, & near his fav'rite Tree;
 "Another came; nor yet beside the Rill,
 "Nor up the Lawn, nor at the Wood was he.

 "The next with Dirges due in sad Array
 "Slow thro' the Churchway Path we saw him born.
 "Approach & read, for thou canst read, the Lay
 "Graved on the Scene beneath yon aged Thorn.

            Epitaph.   1. Son of Earth

E L E G Y

WRITTEN IN A

COUNTRY   CHURCH-YARD.

The Curfew tolls * the knell of parting day,
The lowing herd wind slowly o'er the lea,
The plowman homeward plods his weary way,
And leaves the world to darkness and to me.

Now fades the glimmering landscape on the sight,
And all the air a solemn stillness holds,
Save where the beetle wheels his droning flight,
And drowsy tinklings lull the distant folds ;

Save that from yonder ivy-mantled tow'r
The mopeing owl does to the moon complain   10
Of such, as wand'ring near her secret bow'r,
Molest her ancient solitary reign.

> * ————squilla di lontano,
> Che paia 'l giorno pianger, che si muore.
> *Dante.   Purgat.* [*Canto*] 8.

Beneath those rugged elms, that yew-tree's shade,
Where heaves the turf in many a mould'ring heap,
Each in his narrow cell for ever laid,
The rude Forefathers of the hamlet sleep.

The breezy call of incense-breathing Morn,
The swallow twitt'ring from the straw-built shed,
The cock's shrill clarion, or the echoing horn,
No more shall rouse them from their lowly bed.   20

For them no more the blazing hearth shall burn,
Or busy housewife ply her evening care :
No children run to lisp their sire's return,
Or climb his knees the envied kiss to share.

Oft did the harvest to their sickle yield,
Their furrow oft the stubborn glebe has broke ;
How jocund did they drive their team afield !
How bow'd the woods beneath their sturdy stroke !

Let not Ambition mock their useful toil,
Their homely joys, and destiny obscure ;   30
Nor Grandeur hear with a disdainful smile,
The short and simple annals of the poor.

The boast of heraldry, the pomp of pow'r,
And all that beauty, all that wealth e'er gave,
Awaits alike th' inevitable hour.
The paths of glory lead but to the grave.

Nor you, ye Proud, impute to These the fault,
If Mem'ry o'er their Tomb no Trophies raise,
Where thro' the long-drawn isle and fretted vault
The pealing anthem swells the note of praise.   40

Can storied urn or animated bust
Back to its mansion call the fleeting breath ?
Can Honour's voice provoke the silent dust,
Or Flatt'ry sooth the dull cold ear of Death ?

Perhaps in this neglected spot is laid
Some heart once pregnant with celestial fire ;
Hands, that the rod of empire might have sway'd,
Or wak'd to extasy the living lyre.

But Knowledge to their eyes her ample page
Rich with the spoils of time did ne'er unroll ;   50
Chill Penury repress'd their noble rage,
And froze the genial current of the soul.

Full many a gem of purest ray serene,
The dark unfathom'd caves of ocean bear :
Full many a flower is born to blush unseen,
And waste its sweetness on the desert air.

Some village-Hampden, that with dauntless breast
The little Tyrant of his fields withstood ;
Some mute inglorious Milton here may rest,
Some Cromwell guiltless of his country's blood.　　60

Th' applause of list'ning senates to command,
The threats of pain and ruin to despise,
To scatter plenty o'er a smiling land,
And read their hist'ry in a nation's eyes,

Their lot forbad : nor circumscrib'd alone
Their growing virtues, but their crimes confin'd ;
Forbad to wade through slaughter to a throne,
And shut the gates of mercy on mankind,

The struggling pangs of conscious truth to hide,
To quench the blushes of ingenuous shame,　　70
Or heap the shrine of Luxury and Pride
With incense kindled at the Muse's flame.

Far from the madding crowd's ignoble strife,
Their sober wishes never learn'd to stray;
Along the cool sequester'd vale of life
They kept the noiseless tenor of their way.

Yet ev'n these bones from insult to protect
Some frail memorial still erected nigh,
With uncouth rhimes and shapeless sculpture deck'd,
Implores the passing tribute of a sigh.   80

Their name, their years, spelt by th' unletter'd muse,
The place of fame and elegy supply:
And many a holy text around she strews,
That teach the rustic moralist to die.

For who to dumb Forgetfulness a prey,
This pleasing anxious being e'er resign'd,
Left the warm precincts of the chearful day,
Nor cast one longing ling'ring look behind?

On some fond breast the parting soul relies,
Some pious drops the closing eye requires;   90
Ev'n from the tomb the voice of Nature cries,
* Ev'n in our Ashes live their wonted Fires.

> * Ch'i veggio nel pensier, dolce mio fuoco,
> Fredda una lingua, & due begli occhi chiusi
> Rimaner doppo noi pien di faville.
>
> *Petrarch. Son.* 169.

For thee, who mindful of th' unhonour'd Dead
Dost in these lines their artless tale relate ;
If chance, by lonely contemplation led,
Some kindred Spirit shall inquire thy fate,

Haply some hoary-headed Swain may say,
' Oft have we seen him at the peep of dawn
' Brushing with hasty steps the dews away
' To meet the sun upon the upland lawn.   100

' There at the foot of yonder nodding beech
' That wreathes its old fantastic roots so high,
' His listless length at noontide would he stretch,
' And pore upon the brook that babbles by.

' Hard by yon wood, now smiling as in scorn,
' Mutt'ring his wayward fancies he would rove,
' Now drooping, woeful wan, like one forlorn,
' Or craz'd with care, or cross'd in hopeless love.

' One morn I miss'd him on the custom'd hill,
' Along the heath and near his fav'rite tree ;   110
' Another came ; nor yet beside the rill,
' Nor up the lawn, nor at the wood was he ;

' The next with dirges due in sad array
' Slow thro' the church-way path we saw him born.
' Approach and read (for thou can'st read) the lay,
' Grav'd on the stone beneath yon aged thorn.'

The EPITAPH.

Here rests his head upon the lap of Earth
A Youth to Fortune and to Fame unknown.
Fair Science frown'd not on his humble birth,
And Melancholy mark'd him for her own.   120

Large was his bounty, and his soul sincere,
Heav'n did a recompence as largely send :
He gave to Mis'ry all he had, a tear,
He gain'd from Heav'n ('twas all he wish'd) a friend.

No farther seek his merits to disclose,
Or draw his frailties from their dread abode,
(* There they alike in trembling hope repose,)
The bosom of his Father and his God.

*   ——paventosa speme.   *Petrarch. Son.* 114.

H

DESIGNS

BY

Mr. R. BENTLEY,

FOR SIX

POEMS

BY

Mr. T. GRAY.

LONDON:

Printed for R. DODSLEY, in Pall-mall.

MDCCLIII.

[Lady Cobham, then living at Stoke Poges, after reading the *Elegy* was anxious to make Gray's acquaintance. Miss Speed and Lady Schaub, who were staying with her, brought this about by calling on the poet. They found him out, but Gray returned the call and so the acquaintance began. Gray wrote an account of this first visit, which he called 'A Long Story'. The MS. at Pembroke is dated August 1750; the poem cannot have been finished before October, because of the allusion to Macleane in line 120. It was only once published with Gray's authority in his lifetime, in the *Six Poems* with Bentley's Designs in 1753, from which the present text is taken and from which Bentley's sketch drawing of Stoke Manor, after a rough sketch by Gray, is reproduced. It was also printed in the Dublin edition of 1768.]

A Long STORY.

In Britain's Isle, no matter where,
An ancient pile of building stands :
The Huntingdons and Hattons there
Employ'd the power of Fairy hands

To raise the cieling's fretted height,
Each pannel in achievements cloathing,
Rich windows that exclude the light,
And passages, that lead to nothing.

Full oft within the spatious walls,
When he had fifty winters o'er him,
My grave * Lord-Keeper led the Brawls ;
The Seal, and Maces, danc'd before him.

10

* Hatton, prefer'd by Queen Elizabeth for his graceful Person
and fine Dancing.

His bushy beard, and shoe-strings green,
His high-crown'd hat, and sattin-doublet,
Mov'd the stout heart of England's Queen,
Tho' Pope and Spaniard could not trouble it

What, in the very first beginning !
Shame of the versifying tribe !
Your Hist'ry whither are you spinning ?
Can you do nothing but describe ?   20

A House there is, (and that's enough)
From whence one fatal morning issues
A brace of Warriors, not in buff,
But rustling in their silks and tissues.

The first came cap-a-pee from France
Her conqu'ring destiny fulfilling,
Whom meaner Beauties eye askance,
And vainly ape her art of killing,

The other Amazon kind Heaven
Had arm'd with spirit, wit, and satire :   30
But COBHAM had the polish given,
And tip'd her arrows with good-nature.

To celebrate her eyes, her air - - - - -
Coarse panegyricks would but teaze her.
Melissa is her Nom de Guerre.
Alas, who would not wish to please **her**!

With bonnet blue and capucine,
And aprons long they hid their armour,
And veil'd their weapons bright and keen
In pity to the country-farmer.   40

Fame in the shape of Mr. P - - - t
(By this time all the Parish know it)
Had told, that thereabouts there lurk'd
A wicked Imp they call a Poet,

Who prowl'd the country far and near,
Bewitch'd the children of the peasants,
Dried up the cows, and lam'd the deer,
And suck'd the eggs, and kill'd the pheasants.

My Lady heard their joint petition,
Swore by her coronet and ermine,   50
She'd issue out her high commission
To rid the manour of such vermin.

The Heroines undertook the task,
Thro' lanes unknown, o'er stiles they ventur'd,
Rap'd at the door, nor stay'd to ask,
But bounce into the parlour enter'd.

The trembling family they daunt,
They flirt, they sing, they laugh, they tattle,
Rummage his Mother, pinch his Aunt,
And up stairs in a whirlwind rattle.　　　　60

Each hole and cupboard they explore,
Each creek and cranny of his chamber,
Run hurry-skurry round the floor,
And o'er the bed and tester clamber,

Into the Drawers and China pry,
Papers and books, a huge Imbroglio !
Under a tea-cup he might lie,
Or creased, like dogs-ears, in a folio.

On the first marching of the troops
The Muses, hopeless of his pardon,　　　　70
Convey'd him underneath their hoops
To a small closet in the garden.

So Rumor says.   (Who will, believe.)
But that they left the door a-jarr,
Where, safe and laughing in his sleeve,
He heard the distant din of war.

Short was his joy.   He little knew,
The power of Magick was no fable.
Out of the window, whisk, they flew,
But left a spell upon the table.   80

The words too eager to unriddle
The Poet felt a strange disorder :
Transparent birdlime form'd the middle,
And chains invisible the border.

So cunning was the Apparatus,
The powerful pothooks did so move him,
That, will he, nill he, to the Great-house
He went, as if the Devil drove him.

Yet on his way (no sign of grace,
For folks in fear are apt to pray)   90
To Phœbus he prefer'd his case,
And beg'd his aid that dreadful day.

The Godhead would have back'd his quarrel,
But with a blush on recollection
Own'd, that his quiver and his laurel
'Gainst four such eyes were no protection.

The Court was sate, the Culprit there,
Forth from their gloomy mansions creeping
The Lady *Janes* and *Joans* repair,
And from the gallery stand peeping :   100

Such as in silence of the night
Come (sweep) along some winding entry
(* *Styack* has often seen the sight)
Or at the chappel-door stand sentry ;

In peaked hoods and mantles tarnish'd,
Sour visages, enough to scare ye,
High Dames of honour once, that garnish'd
The drawing-room of fierce Queen Mary !

The Peeress comes.   The Audience stare,
And doff their hats with due submission :   110
She curtsies, as she takes her chair.
To all the People of condition.

* The House-Keeper.

The Bard with many an artful fib,
Had in imagination fenc'd him,
Disproved the arguments of * Squib,
And all that † Groom could urge against him.

But soon his rhetoric forsook him,
When he the solemn hall had seen ;
A sudden fit of ague shook him,
He stood as mute as poor ‡ Macleane.   120

Yet something he was heard to mutter,
' How in the park beneath an old-tree
' (Without design to hurt the butter,
' Or any malice to the poultry,)

' He once or twice had pen'd a sonnet ;
' Yet hoped, that he might save his bacon :
' Numbers would give their oaths upon it,
' He ne'er was for a conj'rer taken.

The ghostly Prudes with hagged face
Already had condemn'd the sinner.   130
My Lady rose, and with a grace - - - -
She smiled, and bid him come to dinner.

* Groom of the Chambers.
† The Steward.
‡ A famous Highwayman hang'd the week before.

' Jesu-Maria ! Madam Bridget,
' Why, what can the Vicountess mean ?
(Cried the square Hoods in woful fidget)
' The times are alter'd quite and clean !

' Decorum's turn'd to mere civility ;
' Her air and all her manners shew it.
' Commend me to her affability !
' Speak to a Commoner and Poet !   140

      (*Here* 500 *Stanzas are lost.*)

And so God save our noble King,
And guard us from long-winded Lubbers,
That to eternity would sing,
And keep my Lady from her Rubbers.

O D E

FOR

M U S I C.

[Through the influence of the Duke of Grafton, Gray had
obtained, in July 1768, the chair of Regius Professor of Modern
History at Cambridge. When, therefore, the Duke was ap-
pointed Chancellor of the University in November, he wrote
the ode to be performed at the installation. It was completed
in April 1769, and is the last of Gray's metrical compositions.
The full title which was appended to the first edition, published
at Cambridge in 1769, is : *Ode performed in the Senate-House
at Cambridge, July 1, 1769, At the Installation of his Grace
Augustus-Henry Fitzroy, Duke of Grafton, Chancellor of the
University. Set to Music by Dr. Randal, Professor of Music.*
(Gray's name is not on the title-page.) The text here printed is
taken from this edition.]

AIR.

" HENCE, avaunt, ('tis holy ground)

" Comus, and his midnight-crew,

" And Ignorance with looks profound,

" And dreaming Sloth of pallid hue,

" Mad Sedition's cry profane,

" Servitude that hugs her chain,

" Nor in these consecrated bowers

" Let painted Flatt'ry hide her serpent-train in flowers.

CHORUS.

" Nor Envy base, nor creeping Gain

" Dare the Muse's walk to stain,   10

" While bright-eyed Science watches round :

" Hence, away, 'tis holy Ground !

RECITATIVE.

From yonder realms of empyrean day

Bursts on my ear th' indignant lay :

There sit the sainted Sage, the Bard divine,

The Few, whom Genius gave to shine

Through every unborn age, and undiscovered clime.

Rapt in celestial transport they,   (*accomp.*)

Yet hither oft a glance from high

They send of tender sympathy   20

To bless the place, where on their opening soul

First the genuine ardor stole.

'Twas *Milton* struck the deep-toned shell,

And, as the choral warblings round him swell,

Meek *Newton's* self bends from his state sublime,

And nods his hoary head, and listens to the rhyme.

AIR.

" Ye brown o'er-arching Groves,

" That Contemplation loves,

" Where willowy *Camus* lingers with delight !

" Oft at the blush of dawn   30

" I trod your level lawn,

" Oft woo'd the gleam of *Cynthia* silver-bright

" In cloisters dim, far from the haunts of Folly,

" With Freedom by my Side, and soft-ey'd Melancholy.

RECITATIVE.

But hark ! the portals sound, and pacing forth

With solemn steps and slow

High Potentates and Dames of royal birth

And mitred Fathers in long order go :

Great *Edward* with the lillies on his brow

From haughty *Gallia* torn,   40

And sad *Chatillon*, on her bridal morn

That wept her bleeding Love, and princely *Clare*,

And *Anjou's* Heroïne, and the paler Rose,

The rival of her crown, and of her woes,

And either *Henry* there,

The murther'd Saint, and the majestic Lord,

That broke the bonds of *Rome*.

(Their tears, their little triumphs o'er,   (*accomp.*)
Their human passions now no more,
Save Charity, that glows beyond the tomb)   50
All that on *Granta's* fruitful plain
Rich streams of regal bounty pour'd,
And bad these aweful fanes and turrets rise,
To hail their *Fitzroy's* festal morning come ;
And thus they speak in soft accord
The liquid language of the skies.

QUARTETTO.

" What is Grandeur, what is Power ?
" Heavier toil, superior pain.
" What the bright reward we gain ?
" The grateful mem'ry of the Good.   60
" Sweet is the breath of vernal shower,
" The bee's collected treasures sweet,
" Sweet music's melting fall, but sweeter yet
" The still small voice of Gratitude.

RECITATIVE.

Foremost and leaning from her golden cloud
The venerable *Marg'ret* see !
" Welcome, my noble Son, (she cries aloud)
" To this, thy kindred train, and me :

" Pleas'd in thy lineaments we trace

" A *Tudor's* fire, a *Beaufort's* grace.   70

AIR.

" Thy liberal heart, thy judging eye,

" The flower unheeded shall descry,

" And bid it round heaven's altars shed

" The fragrance of it's blushing head :

" Shall raise from earth the latent gem

" To glitter on the diadem.

RECITATIVE.

" Lo, *Granta* waits to lead her blooming band,

" Not obvious, not obtrusive, She

" No vulgar praise, no venal incense flings ;

" Nor dares with courtly tongue refin'd   80

" Profane thy inborn royalty of mind :

" She reveres herself and thee.

" With modest pride to grace thy youthful brow

" The laureate wreath, that *Cecil* wore, she brings,

" And to thy just, thy gentle hand

" Submits the Fasces of her sway,

" While Spirits blest above and Men below

" Join with glad voice the loud symphonious lay.

I

GRAND CHORUS.

" Thro' the wild waves as they roar

" With watchful eye and dauntless mien   90

" Thy steady course of honor keep,

" Nor fear the rocks, nor seek the shore :

" The Star of *Brunswick* smiles serene,

" And gilds the horrors of the deep.

ON L⟨OR⟩D H⟨OLLAN⟩Dˢ SEAT
NEAR M⟨ARGAT⟩E, K⟨EN⟩T.

[These verses were written in 1768 when Gray was staying with the Rev. William Robinson at Denton in Kent (see *Correspondence*, Appendix T). According to Mitford, they were found in the drawer of his dressing-table after his departure. There is a copy in Wharton's handwriting among the Egerton MS. 2400 f. 232, from which the text is now printed. The verses were printed anonymously and without Gray's permission in *The New Foundling Hospital for Wit* (1769). The version printed by Mitford is that published by Stephen Jones in 1800.]

OLD and abandon'd by each venal friend

    Here H⟨olland⟩ took the pious resolution

To smuggle some few years and strive to mend

    A broken character and constitution.

On this congenial spot he fix'd his choice,

    Earl Godwin trembled for his neighbouring sand,

Here Seagulls scream and cormorants rejoice,

    And Mariners tho' shipwreckt dread to land,

Here reign the blustring north and blighting east,

    No tree is heard to whisper, bird to sing,   10

Yet nature cannot furnish out the feast,

    Art he invokes new horrors still to bring :

Now mouldring fanes and battlements arise,

   Arches and turrets nodding to their fall,

Unpeopled palaces delude his eyes,

   And mimick desolation covers all.

Ah, said the sighing Peer, had Bute been true

   Nor Shelburn's, Rigby's, Calcraft's friendship vain,

Far other scenes than these had bless'd our view

   And realis'd the ruins that we feign.

Purg'd by the sword and beautifyed by fire,

   Then had we seen proud London's hated walls,

Owls might have hooted in Sᵗ Peters Quire,

   And foxes stunk and litter'd in Sᵗ Pauls.

[Wharton wrote 'Calcrofts'.]

POSTHUMOUS

POEMS.

AGRIPPINA.

A FRAGMENT OF A TRAGEDY.

[Gray sent to West about the end of March 1742 the last speech
of Agrippina in the first scene. In December 1746 he sent 'a scene
in a tragedy' to Walpole, and in January 1747 the rest of the scene
'in an outrageous long speech'. No MS. of *Agrippina* is known to
exist. Mason, who first printed it, altered the text by putting
part of Agrippina's long speech 'into the mouth of Aceronia,
and by breaking it in a few other places'. Tovey cut out what
were obviously Mason's interpolations and conjecturally restored
Gray's text; his version is here followed. Mason put together the
Argument 'from two detached papers' of Gray.]

DRAMATIS PERSONÆ.

AGRIPPINA, the Empress-mother.
NERO, the Emperor.
POPPÆA, believed to be in love with OTHO.
OTHO, a young man of quality, in love with POPPÆA.
SENECA, the Emperor's Preceptor.
ANICETUS, Captain of the Guards.
DEMETRIUS, the Cynic, friend to SENECA.
ACERONIA, Confidant to AGRIPPINA.

SCENE.—*The Emperor's villa at Baiæ.*

THE ARGUMENT.

The drama opens with the indignation of Agrippina at receiv-
ing her son's orders from Anicetus to remove from Baiæ, and
to have her guard taken from her. At this time Otho having
conveyed Poppæa from the house of her husband Rufus Cris-
pinus, brings her to Baiæ, where he means to conceal her among

the crowd; or, if his fraud is discovered, to have recourse to
the Emperor's authority; but, knowing the lawless temper of
Nero, he determines not to have recourse to that expedient
but on the utmost necessity. In the meantime he commits
her to the care of Anicetus, whom he takes to be his friend,
and in whose age he thinks he may safely confide. Nero is
not yet come to Baiæ: but Seneca, whom he sends before
him, informs Agrippina of the accusation concerning Rubellius
Plancus, and desires her to clear herself, which she does briefly:
but demands to see her son, who, on his arrival, acquits her of
all suspicion, and restores her to her honours.

In the meanwhile, Anicetus, to whose care Poppæa had
been intrusted by Otho, contrives the following plot to ruin
Agrippina: he betrays his trust to Otho, and brings Nero, as
it were by chance, to the sight of the beautiful Poppæa; the
Emperor is immediately struck with her charms, and she, by
a feigned resistance, increases his passion: though, in reality,
she is from the first dazzled with the prospect of empire, and
forgets Otho: she therefore joins with Anicetus in his design
of ruining Agrippina, soon perceiving that it will be for her
interest. Otho hearing that the Emperor had seen Poppæa,
is much enraged; but not knowing that this interview was
obtained through the treachery of Anicetus, is readily per-
suaded by him to see Agrippina in secret, and acquaint her
with his fears that her son Nero would marry Poppæa. Agrippina, to support her own power, and to wean the Emperor
from the love of Poppæa, gives Otho encouragement, and
promises to support him. Anicetus secretly introduces Nero
to hear their discourse; who resolves immediately on his
mother's death, and, by Anicetus's means, to destroy her by
drowning. A solemn feast, in honour of their reconciliation,
is to be made; after which she being to go by sea to Bauli, the
ship is so contrived as to sink or crush her; she escapes by
accident, and returns to Baiæ.

In this interval Otho has an interview with Poppæa; and

being duped a second time by Anicetus and her, determines
to fly with her into Greece, by means of a vessel which is to
be furnished by Anicetus ; but he, pretending to remove
Poppæa on board in the night, conveys her to Nero's apart-
ment : she then encourages and determines Nero to banish
Otho, and finish the horrid deed he had attempted on his
mother. Anicetus undertakes to execute his resolves ; and,
under pretence of a plot upon the Emperor's life, is sent with
a guard to murder Agrippina, who is still at Baiæ in imminent
fear, and irresolute how to conduct herself. The account of
her death, and the Emperor's horror and fruitless remorse,
finishes the drama [Mason].

ACT I. SCENE I.

AGRIPPINA. ACERONIA.

Agrip. 'Tis well, begone ! your errand is perform'd.

[*Speaks as to* Anicetus *entering.*

The message needs no comment. Tell your master,

His mother shall obey him. Say you saw her

Yielding due reverence to his high command :

Alone, unguarded and without a lictor

As fits the daughter of Germanicus.

Say, she retir'd to Antium ; there to tend

Her household cares, a woman's best employment.

What if you add, how she turn'd pale and trembled :

You think, you spied a tear stand in her eye,   10

And would have dropp'd, but that her pride restrain'd it?

(Go ! you can paint it well) 'twill profit you,
And please the stripling.   Yet 'twould dash his joy
To hear the spirit of Britannicus
Yet walks on earth : at least there are who know
Without a spell to raise, and bid it fire
A thousand haughty hearts, unus'd to shake
When a boy frowns, nor to be lured with smiles
To taste of hollow kindness, or partake
His hospitable board : they are aware   20
Of th' unpledg'd bowl, they love not aconite.

   Acer.   He's gone : and much I hope these walls alone
And the mute air are privy to your passion.
Forgive your servant's fears, who sees the danger
Which fierce resentment cannot fail to raise
In haughty youth, and irritated power.

   Agrip.   And dost thou talk to me, to me of danger,
Of haughty youth and irritated power,
To her that gave it being, her that arm'd
This painted Jove, and taught his novice hand   30
To aim the forked bolt ; while he stood trembling,
Scar'd at the sound, and dazzled with its brightness ?

   'Tis like, thou hast forgot, when yet a stranger
To adoration, to the grateful steam
Of flattery's incense, and obsequious vows
From voluntary realms, a puny boy,

Deck'd with no other lustre, than the blood

Of Agrippina's race, he liv'd unknown

To fame, or fortune ; haply eyed at distance

Some edileship, ambitious of the power   40

To judge of weights and measures ; scarcely dar'd

On expectation's strongest wing to soar

High as the consulate, that empty shade

Of long-forgotten liberty : when I

Oped his young eye to bear the blaze of greatness ;

Shew'd him where empire tower'd, and bade him strike

The noble quarry. Gods ! then was the time

To shrink from danger ; fear might then have worn

The mask of prudence ; but a heart like mine,

A heart that glows with the pure Julian fire,   50

If bright ambition from her craggy seat

Display the radiant prize, will mount undaunted,

Gain the rough heights, and grasp the dangerous honour.

   Acer. Through various life I have pursued your steps,

Have seen your soul, and wonder'd at its daring :

Hence rise my fears. Nor am I yet to learn

How vast the debt of gratitude which Nero

To such a mother owes ; the world, you gave him,

Suffices not to pay the obligation.

   I well remember too (for I was present)   60

When in a secret and dead hour of night,

Due sacrifice perform'd with barb'rous rites
Of mutter'd charms, and solemn invocation,
You bade the Magi call the dreadful powers,
That read futurity, to know the fate
Impending o'er your son : their answer was,
If the son reign, the mother perishes.
Perish (you cried) the mother ! reign the son !
He reigns, the rest is heav'ns ; who oft has bade,
Ev'n when its will seem'd wrote in lines of blood,   70
Th' unthought event disclose a whiter meaning.
Think too how oft in weak and sickly minds
The sweets of kindness lavishly indulg'd
Rankle to gall ; and benefits too great
To be repaid, sit heavy on the soul,
As unrequited wrongs.   The willing homage
Of prostrate Rome, the senate's joint applause,
The riches of the earth, the train of pleasures
That wait on youth, and arbitrary sway :
These were your gift, and with them you bestow'd   80
The very power he has to be ungrateful.

   Agrip.   Thus ever grave and undisturb'd reflection
Pours its cool dictates in the madding ear
Of rage, and thinks to quench the fire it feels not.
Say'st thou I must be cautious, must be silent,
And tremble at the phantom I have raised ?

Carry to him thy timid counsels. He
Perchance may heed 'em : tell him too, that one
Who had such liberal power to give, may still
With equal power resume that gift, and raise   90
A tempest that shall shake her own creation
To its original atoms—tell me ! say
This mighty emperor, this dreaded hero,
Has he beheld the glittering front of war ?
Knows his soft ear the trumpet's thrilling voice,
And outcry of the battle ? Have his limbs
Sweat under iron harness ? Is he not
The silken son of dalliance, nurs'd in ease
And pleasure's flow'ry lap ?—Rubellius lives,
And Sylla has his friends, though school'd by fear   100
To bow the supple knee, and court the times
With shows of fair obeisance ; and a call,
Like mine, might serve belike to wake pretensions
Drowsier than theirs, who boast the genuine blood
Of our imperial house.   [Cannot my nod]
Rouse [up] eight hardy legions, wont to stem
With stubborn nerves the tide, and face the rigour
Of bleak Germania's snows [?] Four, not less brave,
That in Armenia quell the Parthian force
Under the warlike Corbulo, by me   110
Mark'd for their leader : these, by ties confirm'd,

Of old respect and gratitude, are mine.
Surely the Masians too, and those of Egypt,
Have not forgot my sire : the eye of Rome,
And the Prætorian camp have long rever'd,
With custom'd awe, the daughter, sister, wife,
And mother of their Cæsars.

                              Ha ! by Juno,
It bears a noble semblance.   On this base
My great revenge shall rise ; or say we sound
The trump of liberty ; there will not want,   120
Even in the servile senate, ears to own
Her spirit-stirring voice ; Soranus there,
And Cassius ; Vetus too, and Thrasea,
Minds of the antique cast, rough, stubborn souls,
That struggle with the yoke.   How shall the spark
Unquenchable, that glows within their breasts,
Blaze into freedom, when the idle herd
(Slaves from the womb, created but to stare,
And bellow in the Circus) yet will start,
And shake 'em at the name of liberty,   130
Stung by a senseless word, a vain tradition,
As there were magic in it ? Wrinkled beldams
Teach it their grandchildren, as somewhat rare
That anciently appear'd, but when, extends
Beyond their chronicle—oh ! 'tis a cause

To arm the hand of childhood, and rebrace
The slacken'd sinews of time-wearied age.

  Yes, we may meet, ungrateful boy, we may !
Again the buried Genius of old Rome
Shall from the dust uprear his reverend head,   140
Rous'd by the shout of millions : there before
His high tribunal thou and I appear.
Let majesty sit on thy awful brow,
And lighten from thy eye : around thee call
The gilded swarm that wantons in the sunshine
Of thy full favour ; Seneca be there
In gorgeous phrase of labour'd eloquence
To dress thy plea, and Burrhus strengthen it
With his plain soldier's oath, and honest seeming.
Against thee, liberty and Agrippina :   150
The world, the prize ; and fair befall the victors.

  But soft ! why do I waste the fruitless hours
In threats unexecuted ? Haste thee, fly
These hated walls that seem to mock my shame,
And cast me forth in duty to their lord.

  My thought aches at him ; not the basilisk
More deadly to the sight, than is to me
The cool injurious eye of frozen kindness.
I will not meet its poison. Let him feel
Before he sees me. Yes, I will be gone,   160

But not to Antium—all shall be confess'd,
Whate'er the frivolous tongue of giddy fame
Has spread among the crowd ; things, that but whisper'd
Have arch'd the hearer's brow, and riveted
His eyes in fearful extasy : no matter
What ; so't be strange, and dreadful.—Sorceries,
Assassinations, poisonings—the deeper
My guilt, the blacker his ingratitude.

   And you, ye manes of ambition's victims,
Enshrined Claudius, with the pitied ghosts   170
Of the Syllani, doom'd to early death,
(Ye unavailing horrors, fruitless crimes !)
If from the realms of night my voice ye hear,
In lieu of penitence, and vain remorse,
Accept my vengeance. Though by me ye bled,
He was the cause. My love, my fears for him,
Dried the soft springs of pity in my heart,
And froze them up with deadly cruelty.
Yet if your injur'd shades demand my fate,
If murder cries for murder, blood for blood,   180
Let me not fall alone ; but crush his pride,
And sink the traitor in his mother's ruin.   [*Exeunt.*

SCENE II.

OTHO, POPPÆA.

Otho. Thus far we're safe. Thanks to the rosy queen
Of amorous thefts : and had her wanton son
Lent us his wings, we could not have beguil'd
With more elusive speed the dazzled sight
Of wakeful jealousy. Be gay securely ;
Dispel, my fair, with smiles, the tim'rous cloud
That hangs on thy clear brow. So Helen look'd,
So her white neck reclin'd, so was she borne   190
By the young Trojan to his gilded bark
With fond reluctance, yielding modesty,
And oft reverted eye, as if she knew not
Whether she fear'd, or wish'd to be pursued.

*   *   *   *   *

SONNET

ON THE DEATH OF RICHARD WEST.

[The MS. at Pembroke is dated 'at Stoke, Aug. 1742'.]

In vain to me the smileing Mornings shine,
　And redning Phœbus lifts his golden Fire :
The Birds in vain their amorous Descant joyn ;
　Or chearful Fields resume their green Attire :
These Ears, alas ! for other Notes repine,
　A different Object do these Eyes require.
My lonely Anguish melts no Heart, but mine ;
　And in my Breast the imperfect Joys expire.
Yet Morning smiles the busy Race to chear,
　And new-born Pleasure brings to happier Men :　　10
The Fields to all their wonted Tribute bear :
　To warm their little Loves the Birds complain :
I fruitless mourn to him, that cannot hear,
　And weep the more because I weep in vain.

HYMN TO IGNORANCE.

A FRAGMENT.

[Gray returned to Cambridge in October 1742, and this fragment was composed some time before. There is a copy in Mason's handwriting at Pembroke. First printed by Mason.]

HAIL, horrors, hail! ye ever gloomy bowers,
Ye gothic fanes, and antiquated towers,
Where rushy Camus' slowly-winding flood
Perpetual draws his humid train of mud:
Glad I revisit thy neglected reign,
Oh take me to thy peaceful shade again.
But chiefly thee, whose influence breathed from high
Augments the native darkness of the sky;
Ah, Ignorance! soft salutary power!
Prostrate with filial reverence I adore.   10
Thrice hath Hyperion roll'd his annual race,
Since weeping I forsook thy fond embrace.
Oh say, successful dost thou still oppose
Thy leaden ægis 'gainst our ancient foes?
Still stretch, tenacious of thy right divine,
The massy sceptre o'er thy slumb'ring line?

And dews Lethean through the land dispense
To steep in slumbers each benighted sense ?
If any spark of wit's delusive ray
Break out, and flash a momentary day,   20
With damp, cold touch forbid it to aspire,
And huddle up in fogs the dang'rous fire.

   Oh say—she hears me not, but, careless grown,
Lethargic nods upon her ebon throne.
Goddess ! awake, arise ! alas, my fears !
Can powers immortal feel the force of years ?
Not thus of old, with ensigns wide unfurl'd,
She rode triumphant o'er the vanquished world ;
Fierce nations own'd her unresisted might,
And all was Ignorance, and all was Night.   30

   Oh ! sacred Age !   Oh ! Times for ever lost !
(The Schoolman's glory, and the Churchman's boast.)
For ever gone—yet still to Fancy new,
Her rapid wings the transient scene pursue,
And bring the buried ages back to view.

   High on her car, behold the Grandam ride
Like old Sesostris with barbaric pride ;
. . . a team of harness'd monarchs bend

         *   *   *   *   *   *   *

THE ALLIANCE OF EDUCATION AND GOVERNMENT.

A FRAGMENT.

[Gray sent the first fifty-seven lines of this Essay to Wharton on August 19, 1748. It is completed in the MS. at the British Museum in Wharton's handwriting. The whole fragment is preserved in Gray's handwriting at Pembroke, and the text is printed from this MS. From ' hints ' which he found among Gray's papers, Mason pieced together the following Commentary.]

THE author's subject being (as we have seen) *The necessary alliance between a good form of government and a good mode of education, in order to produce the happiness of mankind*, the Poem opens with two similes ; an uncommon kind of exordium ; but which I suppose the poet intentionally chose, to intimate the analogical method he meant to pursue in his subsequent reasonings. 1st, He asserts that men without education are like sickly plants in a cold or barren soil (l. 1 to 5, and 8 to 12) ; and, 2dly, he compares them, when unblest with a just and well-regulated government, to plants that will not blossom or bear fruit in an unkindly and inclement air (l. 5 to 9, and l. 13 to 22). Having thus laid down the two propositions he means to prove, he begins by examining into the characteristics which (taking a general view of mankind) all men have in common one with another (l. 22 to 39) ; they covet pleasure and avoid pain (l. 31) ; they feel gratitude for benefits (l. 34) ; they desire to avenge wrongs, which they effect either by force or cunning (l. 35) ; they are linked to each other by their common feelings, and participate in sorrow and in joy (l. 36, 37). If then all the human species agree in so many moral particulars, whence arises the diversity of national characters ? This question the poet puts at line 38, and dilates upon to l. 64. Why, says he, have some nations shown a propensity to commerce and industry ; others to war and rapine ; others to ease and pleasure ? (l. 42 to 46). Why have the northern people overspread, in all ages, and prevailed over the southern ? (l. 46 to 58). Why has Asia been, time out of mind, the seat of despotism, and Europe that of freedom ? (l. 59 to 64). Are we from these instances to imagine men necessarily enslaved to the inconveniences of the climate where they were born ? (l. 64 to 72). Or are we not rather to suppose there is a natural strength in the human mind, that is able to vanquish and break through them ? (l. 72 to 84). It is confest, however, that men receive an early tincture from the situation they are placed in, and the climate which produces them (l. 84 to 88). Thus the inhabitants of the mountains, inured to labour and patience, are naturally trained to war (l. 88 to 96) ; while those of the plain are more open to any attack, and softened by ease and plenty (l. 96 to 99). Again, the Ægyptians, from the nature of their situation, might be the inventors of home navigation, from a necessity of keeping up an intercourse between their towns during the inundation of the Nile (l. 99, to * * * .). Those persons would naturally have the first turn to commerce who inhabited a barren coast like the Tyrians, and were persecuted by some neighbouring tyrant ; or were drove to take refuge on some shoals, like the Venetian and Hollander ; their discovery of some rich island, in the infancy of the world, described. The Tartar, hardened to war by his rigorous climate and pastoral life, and by his disputes for water and herbage in a country without land-marks, as also by skirmishes between his rival clans, was consequently fitted to conquer his rich southern neighbours, whom ease and luxury had enervated : yet this is no proof that liberty and valour may not exist in southern climes, since the Syrians and Carthaginians gave noble instances of both ; and the Arabians carried their conquests as far as the Tartars. Rome also (for many centuries) repulsed those very nations which, when she grew weak, at length demolished her extensive empire * * * *

ESSAY I.

... Πόταγ᾽, ὦ ᾽γαθέ· τὰν γὰρ ἀοιδὰν
Οὔτι πω εἰς Ἀΐδαν γε τὸν ἐκλελάθοντα φυλαξεῖς. Theocrit.

As sickly Plants betray a niggard Earth,
Whose barren Bosom starves her gen'rous Birth
Nor genial Warmth, nor genial Juice retains
Their Roots to feed, and fill their verdant Veins :
And as in Climes, where Winter holds his Reign,
The Soil, tho' fertile, will not teem in vain,
Forbids her Gems to swell, her Shades to rise,
Nor trusts her Blossoms to the churlish Skies.
So draw Mankind in vain the vital Airs,
Unform'd, unfriended, by those kindly Cares,   10
That Health and Vigour to the Soul impart,
Spread the young Thought, and warm the opening Heart
So fond Instruction on the growing Powers
Of Nature idly lavishes her Stores,
If equal Justice with unclouded Face
Smile not indulgent on the rising Race,

And scatter with a free, tho' frugal, Hand
Light golden Showers of Plenty o'er the Land :
But Tyranny has fix'd her Empire there,
To check their tender Hopes with chilling Fear,   20
And blast the blooming Promise of the Year.

 This spacious animated Scene survey
From where the rolling Orb, that gives the Day,
His sable Sons with nearer Course surrounds
To either Pole, and Life's remotest Bounds.
How rude so e'er th' exterior Form we find,
Howe'er Opinion tinge the varied Mind,
Alike to all the Kind impartial Heav'n
The Sparks of Truth and Happiness has given :
With Sense to feel, with Mem'ry to retain,   30
They follow Pleasure, and they fly from Pain ;
Their Judgement mends the Plan their Fancy draws,
Th' Event presages, and explores the Cause.
The soft Returns of Gratitude they know,
By Fraud elude, by Force repell the Foe ;
While mutual Wishes, mutual Woes, endear
The social Smile and sympathetic Tear.

 Say then, thro' Ages by what Fate confined
To different Climes seem different Souls assign'd ?
Here measured Laws and philosophic Ease   40
Fix, and improve the polish'd Arts of Peace.

There Industry and Gain their Vigils keep,
Command the Winds, and tame th' unwilling Deep.
Here Force and hardy Deeds of Blood prevail;
There languid Pleasure sighs in every Gale.
Oft o'er the trembling Nations from afar
Has Scythia breath'd the living Cloud of War;
And, where the deluge burst, with sweepy Sway
Their Arms, their Kings, their Gods were roll'd away.
As oft have issued, Host impelling Host,   50
The blue-eyed Myriads from the Baltic Coast.
The prostrate South to the Destroyer yields
Her boasted Titles and her golden Fields:
With grim Delight the Brood of Winter view
A brighter Day, and heavens of azure Hue,
Scent the new Fragrance of the breathing Rose,
And quaff the pendent Vintage, as it grows.
Proud of the yoke, and pliant to the Rod,
Why yet does Asia dread a Monarch's nod,
While European Freedom still withstands   60
Th' encroaching tide, that drowns her less'ning Lands,
And sees far off with an indignant groan
Her native Plains, and Empires once her own.
Can opener Skies, and Suns of fiercer Flame
O'erpower the Fire that animates our Frame;
As Lamps, that shed at Ev'n a chearful Ray,

Fade and expire beneath the Eye of Day ?
Need we the influence of the Northern Star
To string our Nerves and steel our Hearts to War ?
And, where the Face of Nature laughs around,   70
Must sick'ning Virtue fly the tainted Ground ?
Unmanly Thought ! what Seasons can controul,
What fancied Zone can circumscribe the Soul,
Who, conscious of the Source from whence she springs,
By Reason's light on Resolution's wings,
Spite of her frail Companion, dauntless goes
O'er Libya's Deserts and thro' Zembla's snows ?
She bids each slumb'ring Energy awake,
Another Touch, another Temper take,
Suspends th' inferiour Laws that rule our Clay :   80
The stubborn Elements confess her Sway ;
Their little Wants, their low Desires, refine,
And raise the Mortal to a Height divine.

   Not but the human Fabrick from the Birth
Imbibes a flavour of its parent Earth.
As various Tracts enforce a various Toil,
The Manners speak the Idiom of their Soil.
An Iron-Race the Mountain-Cliffs maintain,
Foes to the gentler Genius of the Plain :
For where unwearied Sinews must be found   90
With sidelong Plough to quell the flinty Ground,

To turn the Torrent's swift-descending Flood,

To brave the Savage rushing from the Wood,

What wonder, if to patient Valour train'd

They guard with Spirit, what by Strength they gain'd ?

And while their rocky Ramparts round they see,

The rough abode of want and liberty,

(As lawless Force from Confidence will grow)

Insult the Plenty of the Vales below ?

What wonder in the sultry Climes, that spread, 100

Where Nile redundant o'er his summer-bed

From his broad bosom life and verdure flings,

And broods o'er Egypt with his wat'ry wings,

If with advent'rous oar and ready sail,

The dusky people drive before the gale :

Or on frail floats to distant cities ride,

That rise and glitter o'er the ambient tide,

STANZAS TO MR. BENTLEY.

[These lines were written in 1752 while Richard Bentley was engaged in preparing the Designs for the *Six Poems*. They were transcribed by Mason in the Commonplace Book. The MS. to which Mason had access had the corner of the last stanza torn off. Both Mason and Mitford attempted to supply the missing words, but it seems best to ignore these additions.]

IN silent gaze the tuneful choir among,
    Half pleas'd, half blushing, let the Muse admire,
While Bentley leads her sister-art along,
    And bids the pencil answer to the lyre

See, in their course, each transitory thought
    Fix'd by his touch a lasting essence take ;
Each dream, in Fancy's airy colouring wrought
    To local symmetry and life awake !

The tardy Rhymes that us'd to linger on,
    To Censure cold, and negligent of Fame,   10
In swifter measures animated run,
    And catch a lustre from his genuine flame.

Ah ! could they catch his strength, his easy grace,
    His quick creation, his unerring line ;
The energy of Pope they might efface,
    And Dryden's harmony submit to mine.

But not to one in this benighted age
  Is that diviner inspiration giv'n,
That burns in Shakespeare's or in Milton's page,
  The pomp and prodigality of Heav'n.   20

As, when conspiring in the Diamond's blaze,
  The meaner gems, that singly charm the sight,
Together dart their intermingled rays,
  And dazzle with a luxury of light.

Enough for me, if to some feeling breast
  My lines a secret sympathy . .
And as their pleasing influence . . .
  A sigh of soft reflection . . . .

ODE ON THE PLEASURE ARISING FROM VICISSITUDE.

A FRAGMENT.

[The title was given by Mason to his own completion of Gray's fragment. The fragment is preserved in a transcript made by Mason in the Commonplace Book at Pembroke, entitled ' Fragment of an ode found amongst Mr. Gray's papers after his decease and here transcribed from the corrected copy '. A note copied by Mason from Gray's pocket-book enables us to date it about 1754–5.
' P. B. 1754 :
Contrast between the Winter Past and coming Spring. Joy owing to that Vicissitude. Many that never feel that delight. Sloth envy Ambition. How much happier the rustic that feels it tho' he knows not how.']

Now the golden Morn aloft
    Waves her dew-bespangled wing ;
With vermeil cheek and whisper soft
    She woo's the tardy spring :
Till April starts, and calls around
The sleeping fragrance from the ground ;
And lightly o'er the living scene
Scatters his freshest, tenderest green.

New-born flocks in rustic dance
 Frisking ply their feeble feet.   10
Forgetful of their wintry trance
 The Birds his presence greet.
But chief the Sky-lark warbles high
His trembling thrilling ecstasy
And, less'ning from the dazzled sight,
Melts into air and liquid light.

[Rise, my soul ! on wings of fire,
 Rise the rapturous choir among ;
Hark ! 'tis nature strikes the lyre,
 And leads the general song :]   20

Yesterday the sullen year
 Saw the snowy whirlwind fly ;
Mute was the musick of the air,
 The Herd stood drooping by :
Their raptures now that wildly flow,
No yesterday, nor morrow know ;
'Tis Man alone that Joy descries
With forward and reverted eyes.

Smiles on past Misfortune's brow
 Soft Reflection's hand can trace ;   30

And o'er the cheek of Sorrow throw
 A melancholy grace ;
While Hope prolongs our happier hour,
Or deepest shades, that dimly lour
And blacken round our weary way,
Gilds with a gleam of distant day.

Still, where rosy Pleasure leads,
 See a kindred Grief pursue ;
Behind the steps that Misery treads,
 Approaching Comfort view :   40
The hues of Bliss more brightly glow,
Chastised by sabler tints of woe ;
And blended form, with artful strife,
The strength and harmony of Life.

See the Wretch, that long has tost
 On the thorny bed of Pain,
At length repair his vigour lost,
 And breathe and walk again :
The meanest flowret of the vale,
The simplest note that swells the gale, 50
The common Sun, the air, and skies,
To him are opening Paradise.

Humble Quiet builds her cell,
   Near the source whence Pleasure flows ;
She eyes the clear chrystalline well,
   And tastes it as it goes.
Far below,   the crowd.

Broad and turbulent it grows

       With resistless sweep
They perish in the boundless deep.   60

Mark where Indolence and Pride,
Softly rolling, side by side,
Their dull, but daily round.

EPITAPH ON MRS. CLERKE.

[The epitaph is on a mural tablet of slate and marble in the church at Beckenham in Kent. A copy (with some variants) was sent in a letter to Bedingfield, January 31, 1758. The inscription is—

JANE CLERKE
Died April 27, 1757. AGED 31.]

Lo ! where this silent marble weeps,
A Friend, a wife, a mother sleeps :
A heart, within whose sacred cell
The peaceful virtues lov'd to dwell.
Affection warm, and faith sincere,
And soft humanity were there.
In agony, in death, resign'd,
She felt the wound she left behind,
Her infant image here below,
Sits smiling on a father's woe :   10
Whom what awaits, while yet he strays
Along the lonely vale of days ?
A pang, to secret sorrow dear ;
A sigh ; an unavailing tear ;
Till time shall every grief remove,
With life, with memory, and with love.

EPITAPH ON A CHILD.

[It is reasonably assumed that this is the epitaph which Gray wrote in 1758 for Dr. Wharton, whose eldest son died in infancy. It is reproduced here as it was first printed by Sir Edmund Gosse from a copy made by Alexander Dyce when the original MS. was sold in 1854. There are two copies among the Mitford MSS. at the British Museum, the first of which, Mitford notes, was transcribed from a manuscript in Gray's writing.]

HERE, freed from pain, secure from misery, lies

A child, the darling of his parents' eyes :

A gentler Lamb ne'er sported on the plain,

A fairer flower will never bloom again :

Few were the days allotted to his breath ;

Now let him sleep in peace his night of death.

SKETCH OF HIS OWN CHARACTER.

WRITTEN IN 1761, AND FOUND IN ONE OF HIS
POCKET-BOOKS.

[Mason's transcript is in the Commonplace Book.]

Too poor for a bribe, and too proud to importune,
He had not the method of making a fortune:
Could love, and could hate, so was thought somewhat odd;
No very great wit, he believed in a God:
A place or a pension he did not desire,
But left church and state to Charles Townshend and
Squire.

EPITAPH ON SIR WILLIAM WILLIAMS.

[Sir William Williams was killed in the siege of Belle-Ile in 1761. Gray was asked to write an epitaph for a monument to be erected at Belle-Ile. There is a transcript by Mason in the Pembroke MS. The epitaph was sent to him in a letter of August 1761 for his criticism. But the text printed by Mason in his edition of Gray's *Poems* differs from the copy in the correspondence and from his transcript. The text now printed is that of the letter to Mason.]

HERE, foremost in the dang'rous paths of fame,
    Young Williams fought for England's fair renown ;
His mind each Muse, each Grace adorn'd his frame,
    Nor Envy dared to view him with a frown.

At Aix, uncall'd his maiden-sword he drew,
    (There first in blood his infant glory seal'd)
From fortune, pleasure, science, love, he flew,
    And scorn'd repose, when Britain took the field.

With eyes of flame and cool intrepid breast,
    Victor he stood on Belleisle's rocky steeps :   10
Ah gallant Youth ! this marble tells the rest,
    Where melancholy Friendship bends and weeps.

THE DEATH OF HOEL.

FROM ANEURIN, MONARCH OF THE BARDS, EXTRACTED
FROM THE GODODIN.

[There is a copy in Gray's handwriting at Pembroke. The
poem was probably written about the same time as the *Triumphs
of Owen.*]

HAD I but the torrent's might,
With headlong rage and wild affright
Upon Deïra's squadrons hurl'd,
To rush, and sweep them from the world !

Too, too secure in youthful pride,
By them my friend, my Hoel, died,
Great Cian's son : of Madoc old
He ask'd no heaps of hoarded gold ;
Alone in Nature's wealth array'd,
He ask'd and had the lovely maid.   10

To Cattraeth's vale in glitt'ring row
Thrice two hundred Warriors goe ;
Every Warrior's manly neck
Chains of regal honour deck,

Wreath'd in many a golden link :
From the golden cup they drink
Nectar, that the bees produce,
Or the grape's ecstatic juice.
Flush'd with mirth and hope they burn :
But none from Cattraeth's vale return,   20
Save Aeron brave, and Conan strong,
(Bursting thro' the bloody throng)
And I, the meanest of them all,
That live to weep, and sing their fall.

CARADOC.

[This and the following fragment, which were printed in Mason's edition of Gray's Poems, are also taken from the *Gododin* of Aneurin.]

HAVE ye seen the tusky boar,
Or the bull, with sullen roar,
On surrounding foes advance ?
So Caràdoc bore his lance.

CONAN.

CONAN'S name, my lay, rehearse,
Build to him the lofty verse,
Sacred tribute of the bard,
Verse, the hero's sole reward.
As the flame's devouring force ;
As the whirlwind in its course ;
As the thunder's fiery stroke,
Glancing on the shiver'd oak ;
Did the sword of Conan mow
The crimson harvest of the foe.

10

THE CANDIDATE.

[John Montagu, fourth Earl of Sandwich, known by the nickname of Jemmy Twitcher from the character in *The Beggar's Opera*, was a candidate for the office of High Steward of the University of Cambridge in 1764. Gray no doubt wrote these verses at the time of the Election, and must have sent a copy to Walpole. It is probable that they were printed by Walpole at the Strawberry Hill Press some years after Gray's death (see *Correspondence*, Appendix P). There are two copies of the leaflet at Eton, from one of which the text is now printed.]

WHEN sly Jemmy Twitcher had smugg'd up his face

With a lick of court white-wash, and pious grimace,

A wooing he went, where three Sisters of old

In harmless society guttle and scold.

Lord ! Sister, says Physic to Law, I declare

Such a sheep-biting look, such a pick-pocket air,

Not I, for the Indies ! you know I'm no prude ;

But his nose is a shame, and his eyes are so lewd !

Then he shambles and straddles so oddly, I fear—

No ; at our time of life, 'twould be silly, my dear.   10

I don't know, says Law, now methinks, for his look,

'Tis just like the picture in Rochester's book.

But his character, Phyzzy, his morals, his life ;
When she died, I can't tell, but he once had a wife.

They say he's no Christian, loves drinking and whoring,
And all the town rings of his swearing and roaring,
His lying, and filching, and Newgate-bird tricks :—
Not I,—for a coronet, chariot and six.

Divinity heard, between waking and dozing,
Her sisters denying, and Jemmy proposing ;   20
From dinner she rose with her bumper in hand,
She stroked up her belly, and stroked down her band.

What a pother is here about wenching and roaring !
Why David loved catches, and Solomon whoring.
Did not Israel filch from th' Ægyptians of old
Their jewels of silver, and jewels of gold ?
The prophet of Bethel, we read, told a lie :
He drinks ; so did Noah : he swears ; so do I.
To refuse him for such peccadillos, were odd ;
Besides, he repents, and he talks about G--.   30

Never hang down your head, you poor penitent elf !
Come, buss me, I'll be Mrs. Twitcher myself.
D - - n ye both for a couple of Puritan bitches !
He's Christian enough, that repents, and that ••-••----.

VERSES FROM SHAKESPEARE.

[These lines were sent to Mason in a letter of about July 8, 1765. The first draft is in a notebook of Gray's owned by Lt.-Col. Sir John Murray. See Dr. Toynbee's note in *Modern Language Review*, Jan. 1930, p. 83. The text printed here is that of the letter. There is a copy among the Mitford MSS. with a few variations.]

WILLIAM SHAKESPEARE to Mrs ANNE, Regular Servant to the Revd Mr PRECENTOR of York.

A MOMENT's patience, gentle Mistris Anne !
(But stint your clack for sweet St Charitie)
'Tis Willy begs, once a right proper Man,
Tho' now a Book, and interleav'd, you see.

  Much have I born from canker'd Critick's spite,
From fumbling Baronets, and Poets small,
Pert Barristers, & Parsons nothing bright :
But, what awaits me now, is worst of all !

  'Tis true, our Master's temper natural
Was fashion'd fair in meek & dovelike guise :   10
But may not honey's self be turn'd to gall
By residence, by marriage, & sore eyes ?

If then he wreak on me his wicked will :
Steal to his closet at the hour of prayer,
And (when thou hear'st the organ piping shrill)
Grease his best pen, & all he scribbles, tear.

Better to bottom tarts & cheesecakes nice,
Better the roast-meat from the fire to save,
Better be twisted into caps for spice,
Than thus be patch'd, & cobbled in one's grave !   20

So York shall taste, what Clouët never knew ;
So from *our* works sublimer fumes shall rise :
While Nancy earns the praise to Shakespear due
For glorious puddings, & immortal pies.

SONG. (1)

[This and the following are said to have been written at the request of Miss Speed, ' that she might possess something from his pen on the subject of love '. The Countess de Viry (Miss Speed) gave them both to the Rev. Mr. Leman in 1780, who passed them on to Joseph Warton. The title ' Amatory Lines ' was given by Mitford in his edition of 1814, but it is simply called ' Song ' in a transcript made by Mason among the Pembroke MSS. Mason notes that the transcript is taken ' from an interlined and corrected copy '. His version has been followed in the text.]

'Midst Beauty and Pleasure's gay triumphs, to languish
And droop without knowing the source of my anguish :
To start from short slumbers, and look for the morning—
Yet close my dull eyes when I see it returning ;

Sighs sudden and frequent, looks ever dejected
Sounds that steal from my tongue, by no meaning
    connected !
Ah say, Fellow-swains, how these symptoms befell me ?
They smile, but reply not. Sure Delia will tell me !

SONG. (2)

[Referring to the song, Walpole wrote to the Countess of Ailesbury, November 28, 1761, ' You will like . . . to see some words which Mr. Gray has writ at Miss Speed's request, to an air of Geminiani : the thought is from the French '. There is a transcript of Mason's at Pembroke from which the text is here printed.]

THYRSIS when we parted swore,

　Ere the spring he would return.

Ah what means yon violet flower,

　And the buds that deck the thorn?

'Twas the Lark that upward sprung!

'Twas the Nightingale that sung!

Idle notes, untimely green,

　Why such unavailing haste?

Western gales, and skies serene

　Prove not always winter past?　　　　　　　10

Cease my doubts, my fears to move;

Spare the honour of my Love.

EPITAPH ON MRS. MASON.

[Mrs. Mason died in May 1767. Mason wrote an epitaph
for a monument erected in Bristol Cathedral. Norton Nicholls
in his 'Reminiscences' published by Mitford in *The Works of
Thomas Gray*, vol. v (1843), stated (pp. 39, 40) that the last four
lines were written by Gray and that he saw them in Gray's
handwriting.]

TELL them, though 'tis an awful thing to die,

('Twas e'en to thee) yet the dread path once trod,

Heaven lifts its everlasting portals high,

And bids the pure in heart behold their God.

SATIRE ON THE HEADS OF HOUSES;

[This satire was first printed by Sir Edmund Gosse from a MS. in the possession of Lord Houghton. There is another copy among the Mitford MSS.]

O CAMBRIDGE, attend
To the Satire I've pen'd
On the Heads of thy Houses,
Thou Seat of the Muses !

Know the Master of Jesus
Does hugely displease us ;
The Master of Maudlin
In the same dirt is dawdling ;
The Master of Sidney
Is of the same kidney ;   10
The Master of Trinity
To him bears affinity ;
As the Master of Keys
Is as like as two pease,
So the Master of Queen's
Is as like as two beans ;

The Master of King's
Copies them in all things;
The Master of Catherine
Takes them all for his pattern;   20
The Master of Clare
Hits them all to a hair;
The Master of Christ
By the rest is enticed;
But the Master of Emmanuel
Follows them like a spaniel;
The Master of Benet
Is of the like tenet;
The Master of Pembroke
Has from them his system took;   30
The Master of Peter's
Has all the same features;
The Master of St. John's
Like the rest of the Dons.

P.S.—As to Trinity Hall
    We say nothing at all.

TOPHET.

[The Rev. Henry Etough is the person alluded to. The lines were written beneath a drawing of Etough made by Mason, probably about the year 1749, which was etched by Mr. Tyson of St. Benet's College in 1769. (See article in the *Times Literary Supplement*, 9 Oct. 1930.) The etching is here reproduced from a copy in the Cole MSS. There is a transcript made by Mason at Pembroke, which has been followed in the text here printed. Lines 3 and 4 are written below the rest in the transcript, and described as ' addition in the first copy ' and marked for insertion after line 2. The verses were printed with the omission of the third and fourth lines in the *Gentleman's Magazine* of October, 1785.]

Such *Tophet* was ; so looked the grinning fiend

While frighted prelates bow'd and called him friend ;

I saw them bow, and while they wish'd him dead,

With servile simper nod the mitred head.

Our Mother-Church with half-averted sight

Blush'd as she blesst her griesly proselyte :

Hosannahs rung through Hell's tremendous borders,

And Satan's self had thoughts of taking orders.

Mr. Etough of Thearsfeild in Hartfordshire.
obiit 1757.

Such Tophet was—so grin'd the bawling Fiend,
While frighted Prelates bow'd and called him friend:
Our Mother Church with half averted sight
Blush'd as she blest her grisly Proselyte.:
Hosannas rung thro' Hell's tremendous Borders
And Satan's self had thoughts of taking orders.

Gray.

WMason delin: Mr Tyson f: aquâ forti: 1769.

THE REV. HENRY ETOUGH

INVITATION TO MASON.

[These lines were sent in a letter to Mason, dated January 8, 1768.]

PRIM *Hurd* attends your call, & *Palgrave* proud,
Stonhewer the lewd, & *Delaval* the loud.
For thee does *Powel* squeeze, & *Marriot* sputter,
And *Glyn* cut phizzes, & Tom *Nevile* stutter.
Brown sees thee sitting on his nose's tip,
The Widow feels thee in her aching hip,
For thee fat *Nanny* sighs, & handy *Nelly*,
And *Balguy* with a Bishop in his belly !

COUPLET ABOUT BIRDS.

[Norton Nicholls in his 'Reminiscences' refers to this couplet: 'Two verses made by Mr. Gray as we were walking in the spring in the neighbourhood of Cambridge'.]

THERE pipes the woodlark, and the song-thrush there
Scatters his loose notes in the waste of air.

PARODY ON AN EPITAPH.

[Wharton notes " Extempore Epitapth on Ann Countess of
Dorset, Pembroke, and Montgomery, made by Mr. Gray on
reading the Epitapth on her mothers [the Countess of Cumberland's] tomb in the Church at Appleby composed by the Countess
in the same manner." Gray must have visited Appleby with
Wharton in September 1767 (see Letter 453, n. 3). The text is
from the autograph copy in Egerton MS. 2400, fol. 181. The
monument was erected in 1617 to Margaret, widow of George
Clifford, third Earl of Cumberland.]

Now clean, now hideous, mellow now, now gruff,

She swept, she hiss'd, she ripen'd & grew rough,

At Broom, Pendragon, Appleby & Brough.

IMPROMPTUS.

[The following lines are taken from Egerton MS. 2400, ff. 233,
234, in Wharton's handwriting at the British Museum.]

Extempore by M^r Gr⟨ay⟩ on Dr. K⟨eene⟩, B⟨ishop⟩ of C⟨hester⟩.

THE Bishop of Chester

Tho' wiser than Nestor

And fairer than Esther,

If you scratch him will fester.

one day the Bishop having offered to give a
Gentleman a Goose⟨,⟩ M^r Gr⟨ay⟩ composed
his Epitapth, thus.

HERE lies Edmund Keene Lord Bishop of Chester,

He eat a fat goose, and could not digest her—

And this upon his Lady—

HERE lies Mrs. Keene the Bishop of Chester,
She had a bad face which did sadly molest her.

Impromptu by Mr Gray going out of Raby Castle.

HERE lives Harry Vane,
Very good claret and fine Champaign

A Couplet by Mr Gray

WHEN you rise from your dinner as light as before
'Tis a sign you have eat just enough and no more.

LINES ON DR. ROBERT SMITH.

[The following lines were written when it was proposed by the Master, Dr. Robert Smith, to cut down the chestnuts at Trinity College.   From being the author of a treatise on optics, he gained the nickname of Old Focus.   They were preserved by Professor Adam Sedgwick and were first printed by Sir Edmund Gosse.]

Do you ask why old Focus Silvanus defies,
    And leaves not a chestnut in being ?
'Tis not that old Focus himself has got eyes,
    But because he has writ about Seeing.

[LINES SPOKEN BY THE GHOST OF JOHN DENNIS AT THE DEVIL TAVERN.

From the autograph letter to Walpole, written at Cambridge December 8, 1734, in the Waller Collection. First printed by Dr. Paget Toynbee in *The Correspondence of Gray, Walpole, West, and Ashton*, vol. i, pp. 12–15. It is the earliest original poem by Gray now extant. Walpole in his memoir of Gray (prefixed to Mitford's edition of *The Correspondence of Gray and Mason*, 1853, p. xxxi) says, ' One of his first pieces of poetry was an answer in English verse to an epistle from H. W.' Gray introduces the verse with a sentence of prose : ' I (tho' I say it) had too much modesty to venture answering your dear, diverting Letter, in the Poetical Strain myself : but, when I was last at the Devil, meeting by chance with the deceased Mr Dennis there, he offer'd his Service, &, being tip'd with a Tester, wrought, what follows— ']

From purling Streams & the Elysian Scene,

From Groves, that smile with never-fading Green

I reascend ; in Atropos' despight

Restored to Celadon, & upper light :

Ye gods, that sway the Regions under ground,

Reveal to mortal View your realms profound ;

At his command admit the eye of Day ;

When Celadon commands, what God can disobey ?

Nor seeks he your Tartarean fires to know,

The house of Torture, & th' Abyss of Woe ;   10

But happy fields & Mansions free from Pain,

Gay Meads, & springing flowers best please ye gentle
   Swain :
  That little, naked, melancholy thing
My Soul, when first she tryed her flight to wing ;
Began with speed new Regions to explore,
And blunder'd thro' a narrow Postern door ;
First most devoutly having said its Prayers,
It tumbled down a thousand pair of [Stairs],
Thro' Entries long, thro' Cellars vast & deep,
Where ghostly Rats their habitations keep,   20
Where Spiders spread their Webs, & owlish Goblins
   sleep.
After so many Chances had befell,
It came into a mead of Asphodel :
Betwixt the Confines of ye light & dark
It lies, of 'Lyzium ye St James's park :
Here Spirit-Beaux flutter along the Mall,
And Shadows in disguise scate o'er ye Iced Canal :
Here groves embower'd, & more sequester'd Shades,
Frequented by ye Ghosts of Ancient Maids,
Are seen to rise : the melancholy Scene   30
With gloomy haunts, & twilight walks between
Conceals the wayward band : here spend their time
Greensickness Girls, that died in youthful prime,
Virgins forlorn, all drest in Willow-green-i

With Queen Elizabeth and Nicolini.

  More to reveal, or many words to use
Would tire alike your patience & my muse.
Believe, that never was so faithful found
Queen Proserpine to Pluto under ground,
Or Cleopatra to her Marc-Antony   40
As Orozmades to his Celadony.
  P:S:
Lucrece for half a crown will shew you fun,
But Mrs Oldfield is become a Nun.
Nobles & Cits, Prince Pluto & his Spouse
Flock to the Ghost of Covent-Garden house :
Plays, which were hiss'd above, below revive ;
When dead applauded, that were damn'd alive :
The People, as in life, still keep their Passions,
But differ something from the world in Fashions.
Queen Artemisia breakfasts on Bohea,   50
And Alexander wears a Ramilie.

NOTES.

ODE ON THE SPRING.

Variations in the MS. copy at Pembroke College, Cambridge :

12. Their broadest brownest shade

19, 20. How low, how indigent the Proud,

        How little are the Great ! (*and so in letter to Walpole,* *Oct.* 1746.)

ODE ON THE DEATH OF A FAVOURITE CAT.

Variations :

On the Death of Selima, a favourite Cat, who fell into a China-Tub with Gold-fishes in it, & was drown'd *is the title given to this Ode in Pembroke MS.* : On a favourite Cat, call'd Selima, that fell, &c. *Wharton MS.*

4, 5. *The lines are transposed in Dodsley's* Collection, 1748.

10. Her] The *Dodsley's* Collection, 1748, *and Foulis edition.*

13. 'midst] 'mid *Pembroke MS.*

14. angel] beauteous *Pembroke MS., and in Dodsley's* Collection, 1748, *and Foulis edition,* 1768.

24. averse to] a foe to *Dodsley's* Collection, 1748.

25. looks] eye *Pembroke MS.* : eyes *Wharton MS.*

35. Susan] Harry *in Wharton MS., and in Dodsley's* Collection, 1748.

36. What fav'rite has a friend ! *Dodsley's* Collection, 1748.

40. tempts] strikes *Pembroke and Wharton MSS.*

ODE ON A DISTANT PROSPECT OF ETON COLLEGE.

Variations in Pembroke MS :

7. Of Grove and Lawn & Mead survey,

22. sprightly] smileing. *So Eton MS.*

26. arm] arms *Foulis edition.*

29. To chase the Hoop's elusive speed,

41, 56. *The motto from Menander is given in the margin.*

55. 'em] them *Eton MS., Foulis edition.*

59. murth'rous] griesly *originally stood, but* murtherous *is given in the margin as a variant.*

60. them] 'em *So Eton MS., Foulis edition.*

71. this] That *So Eton MS.*   75. those] These.

HYMN TO ADVERSITY.

Variations in Pembroke MS.:

Gray added a second motto: Ξυμφέρει

     Σωφρονεῖν ὑπὸ στένει. *Id. Eumenid* : 523.

So in Foulis edition, 1768, *but with misprint* ΣΤΕΝΟΥ.

8. With Pangs unfelt before & Misery not their own.

The second part of this line is struck out in MS. and the reading of the text is inserted above the line.

32. *In margin* ἁ γλυκύδακρυς.

42. Thy milder influence deign to impart.

THE PROGRESS OF POESY.

The Pembroke and Wharton MSS. head each division ' strophe 1 ', ' antistrophe 1 ', *&c.*

1. Awake, my Lyre, my Glory, wake, *Pembroke MS.* (*present reading in margin*).

2. rapture] transport *Pembroke and Wharton MSS.*

10. rowling] rushing *Bedingfield MS.*

11. With torrent-rapture see it pour; *Pembroke and Wharton MSS.*

12. The rocks,] While rocks *Bedingfield MS.*

23. dark] black *Bedingfield, Pembroke, and Wharton MSS.*

34. in] the *Pembroke and Wharton MSS.*

36. their] the *Wharton MS.*

52, 53 :

Till o'er the eastern cliffs from far

Hyperion hurls around his glittering shafts of war.

                     Pembroke MS. (*struck out*).

Till fierce Hyperion from afar
Hurls *at* their *flying* rear his glitt'ring shafts of war.

     on   scatter'd
              shadowy   *In margin of Pembroke MS.*

Till fierce Hyperion from afar
Pours on their scatter'd rear his glitt'ring shafts of war.

                        Wharton MS.

57. shiv'ring] buried *Pembroke MS., but corrected in margin.*
    dull] chill *Pembroke MS., but corrected in margin.*

69. Or] And *Pembroke MS.*

71. Echoes] *Pembroke and Wharton MSS. Walpole printed* Echo's, *which Gray corrects in a letter to him,* August 10, 1757 (*Correspondence*, Letter 243). The error was repeated in Dodsley's edition of 1768.

76. Murmur'd a celestial sound *Pembroke MS., with the later reading in the margin.*

93. Horrour] Terror *Wharton MS. and in the margin of Pembroke MS.*

108. Bright-eyed] Full-plumed *Pembroke and Wharton MSS.*

118–22.   Yet, when they first were open'd on the day,
        Before his visionary eyes would run
        Such Forms, as glitter in the Muse's ray
        With orient hues unborrow'd of the Sun :
        Yet never can he fear a vulgar fate.
       Pembroke MS. (followed by the later reading).

119. forms] shapes *inserted in margin of Pembroke MS.*

THE BARD.

In August 1756 *Gray sent ll.* 25–56 *in a letter to Bedingfield and in May* 1757 *ll.* 115–44 *in a letter to Mason; a little later he sent or gave to Wharton a copy of ll.* 57–144 *with his final corrections written above the line and his earlier versions struck out (see Letter* 205 A).

Variations in the Bedingfield copy : 29 Cadwallo's] Caswallo's ; 30 stormy] roaring ; 31 Brave] Great ; 43 they] ye.

17, 18. *In a letter to Wharton of August* 21, 1755, *Gray accepted Wharton's suggestion to read :*

> With fury pale, and pale with woe,
> Secure of fate, the Poet stood.

but the substitution was not made in the final version.

62. sorrow's . . . solitude] Sorrow's . . . Solitude *Wharton MS. In a letter to Walpole of August* 20, 1757, *Gray pointed out that the words should have had capital letters in the Strawberry Hill edition.*

The variations in ll. 63–110 *are the cancelled readings in the Wharton MS.*

63. Victor] Conqueror   64. his] the

65. no . . . no . . .] What . . . what . . .

69. The Swarm, that hover'd in thy noontide ray

70. Morn] day

71–6. Mirrors of Saxon truth and loyalty,
> Your helpless old expiring master view
> They hear not. scarce Religion dares supply
> Her mutter'd Requiems, & her holy Dew.
> Yet thou, proud Boy, from Pomfret's walls shalt send
> A sigh, & envy oft thy happy Grandsire's end.

The lines as they stand in the text are written at the back of the MS., with in *for* on *in l.* 74.

82. A baleful smile upon] A smile of horror on (*uncorrected*).

87. Ye] Grim

90. holy] hallow'd (*uncorrected*).   101. thus] here

102. Leave your despairing Caradoc to mourn

103. track] clouds   104. melt] sink

105. oh] ah (*uncorrected*).   solemn scenes] scenes of heav'n

106. glitt'ring] golden

109, 110. From Cambria's thousand hills a thousand strains
> Triumphant tell aloud, another Arthur reigns.

111, 112. Youthful [Haughty *Mason*] Knights & Barons bold
> With dazzling helm & horrent spear

Wharton and Mason MSS.

114. In] Of *Mason MS.*

116. of the Briton-Line] born of Arthur's line *Mason MS.*

117. Her ... her ...] A ... an ... *Wharton MS.*

123. calls] wakes *Mason MS.*

128. buskin'd] mystic *Mason MS.*

130. With Horror wild, that chills the throbbing breast.

Mason MS.

144. plung'd] sunk *Wharton and Mason MSS.*

THE FATAL SISTERS.

15. Sword] Blade *Wharton MS.*

17, 18. Sangrida, terrific Maid,
    Mista black, and Hilda see, *Wharton MS.*

23. Blade] Sword *Wharton MS.*

28. triumph] conquer *Pembroke MS.* (*written over* triumph).

31. Gunna and Gondula, spread *Pembroke and Wharton MSS.*

33. slaughter] havock *Pembroke MS.*

44. shall] must *Pembroke and Wharton MSS.*

45. his] her *Pembroke MS.*

50. blot] veil *Wharton MS.*

59. winding] ecchoing *Wharton MS.*

61-3. Sisters, hence ! 'tis time to ride :
    Now your thund'ring faulchion wield ;
    Now your sable steed bestride,
Wharton MS. So Pembroke, but with faulchions *and* steeds.

THE DESCENT OF ODIN.

The following various readings are in the Wharton MS. unless otherwise stated :

11. fruitless] ceaseless

14. shakes] quakes

23. accents] murmurs

27. call] voice

29. my troubled] a weary

35. he] this

41, 42. yon] the *Pembroke and Wharton MSS.*

48. reach] touch

51. Once again] Prophetess

52. Prophetess] Once again

59, 60. Once again my call obey
         Prophetess, arise and say

61 *and* 62 *transposed.*   65. wond'rous] giant

74. awake] arise   77. Who their flowing tresses tear,

79. Tell me] Say from   sorrows] sorrow *Pembroke MS.*

83. The Mightiest of the mighty line   87. hence, and] Odin,

90. has] have   92. Has reassum'd] Reassumes

THE TRIUMPHS OF OWEN.

The following four lines are added at the end of the Pembroke MS.
         Check'd by the torrent-tide of blood
         Backward Meinai rolls his flood :
         While heap'd his Master's feet around
         Prostrate Warriors gnaw the ground.

ELEGY WRITTEN IN A COUNTRY CHURCH-YARD.

The variations in the Eton MS. are not noted here as it is given in full in an appendix.

1. parting] dying *Gray's first thought, as recorded by Norton Nicholls* ('changed . . . to avoid the *concetto*').

2. wind] winds *first edition.*

7. droning] drony *Foulis edition,* 1768.

8. And] Or *Pembroke and Wharton MSS.*

11. secret] sacred *first edition.*

19. or] and *Pembroke and Wharton MSS.*

20. rouse] wake *first edition.*

22. housewife] Huswife *Wharton MS.*

24. Or] Nor *Pembroke and Wharton MSS.*

25. sickle] Sickles *Wharton MS.*

36. paths . . . lead] path . . . leads *Foulis edition.*

37, 38. Forgive, ye Proud, th' involuntary Fault,
          If Memory to These no Trophies raise

These lines are found in this form in all the three MSS. and were so printed in the first edition. In the Pembroke MS. the reading given in the text is added in the margin.

47. rod] Reins *Pembroke and Wharton MSS., but in the former MS.* Rod *is inserted in margin.* Reins *is printed in the first edition.*

68. And] Or *Wharton MS.*

71. shrine] Shrines *Wharton MS.*

82. elegy] Epitaph *Pembroke MS.*

92. Ev'n . . . live] And . . . glow *Pembroke and Wharton MSS. In Pembroke MS. the present reading is given in margin. In the first edition the line read* 'Awake, and faithful to her wonted Fires'.

96. kindred] hidden *first edition.*

105. smiling] frowning *first edition.*

106. he would] would he *Pembroke and Wharton MSS.*

109. on] from *Pembroke MS.*

116. aged] ancient *obliterated in the Pembroke MS. and* aged *written above.*

The following stanza appears in the Eton MS. and at the end of the Pembroke MS. It is not in Wharton MS. It was first printed in the third edition 1751, *and was omitted again in* 1753.

There scatter'd oft, the Earliest of the Year,
    By Hands unseen, are Showers of Violets found :
The Red-breast loves to build, & warble there,
    And little Footsteps lightly print the ground.

A LONG STORY.

Various readings in Pembroke MS. :

10. *Note.* Sr Christ. Hatton, promoted by Queen Elizabeth . . .

41. Mr. Purt

73. (Who will, believe.)] Who will, may believe.

91. prefer'd] explain'd

116. could] might   126. Yet] But

HYMN TO IGNORANCE.

Variations in Mason's transcript :

3. Camus'] Camus

17. O'er all the land Lethean showers dispense

18. To] And

After the asterisks the following line appears in the Mason transcript : 'The pondrous Waggon lumberd slowly on . . .'

THE ALLIANCE OF EDUCATION AND GOVERNMENT.

Various readings in the Wharton MS. :

2. barren] flinty

19. Tyranny has] gloomy Sway have

21. blooming] vernal

55. heavens] Skies   56. Scent] Catch

Mason adds : ' I found also among these papers a single couplet, much too beautiful to be lost though the place where he meant to introduce it cannot be ascertained :

> When love could teach a monarch to be wise,
> And gospel-light first dawned from Bullen's eyes.

ODE ON THE PLEASURE ARISING FROM VICISSITUDE.

The following were noted by Mason as ' Variations in the first copy ' :

10. Frisking] Quaintly

11. Rousd from their long & wintry trance

15. less'ning] towering

17–20. *These lines are omitted in Mason's transcript but are given separately as found in Gray's Pocket-Book. Mason places them here.*

21. sullen] darken'd

22. snowy whirlwind] scowling tempest *and a second variant* snow in whirlwind

29. past] black

53–63. *Not in Mason's transcript, but given separately on the opposite leaf.*

EPITAPH ON MRS. CLERKE.

The following variants are from the Bedingfield MS. :
1. silent] little.   3. The peaceful virtues] Each peaceful Virtue.
7–10. *Mason, in a note to the poem, gives the following lines as a*
MS. variation ' after line 6, in the place of the four next '.

> To hide her cares her only art,
> Her pleasure, pleasures to impart,
> In ling'ring pain, in death resign'd,
> Her latest agony of mind
> Was felt for him, who could not save
> His All from an untimely grave :

EPITAPH ON A CHILD.

1. freed] free *Mitford MS. 2.*   6. his] the *Mitford MS. 2.*

SKETCH OF HIS OWN CHARACTER.

5. place] Post *Pembroke MS. Mason adds an unintelligible note*
' first word *Place* wch authenticates these lines '.
6. Charles Townshend] C—s T—ns—d *Pembroke MS.*

EPITAPH ON SIR WILLIAM WILLIAMS.

5. At Aix his voluntary sword he drew. *Pembroke MS., Mason.*
6. infant] maiden *in Mitford's quotation of ll.* 1, 2, 5, 6 (*B.M.*
Add. MS. 32562, fol. 33).   glory] honour *Pembroke MS., Mason.*
8. And scorn'd] Nor brook'd *given as a variation in Pembroke MS.*
9. intrepid] undaunted *Pembroke MS.* (*with* intrepid *as a*
variation), *Mason.*
12. Where bleeding Friendship o'er her altar weeps.
   Where Montagu and bleeding Friendship weep.
          Alternative variations in Pembroke MS.
Rejected stanza given in Pembroke MS. :
   Warrior, that readst the melancholy line
      .   .   .   .
   Oh be his Genius, be his spirit thine
   And share his Virtues with a happier fate.

VERSES FROM SHAKESPEARE.

*Various readings in (A) the first draft, and (B) the copy among,
the Mitford MSS. :*

2. But] And *A*   your] thy *A, B*   sweet] dear *A*

5. canker'd] crabbed *B*   8. worst of all] worse than all *B*

9. 'Tis . . . master's] True, the Precentor's *A*

10. fashion'd fair] moulded soft *A*   dove-like] lowly *with
alternative* dovelike *A.*

12. sore eyes] mince pies *B*

The fifth stanza is transposed and comes third in B.

17 cheesecakes] puddings *altered to* biscuits *A*

17, 19 *are transposed in A.*

20. one's] my *A*

22. our] thy *altered to* our *A*   works] work *B*

23. earns] reaps *A*

24. For glorious puddings] To glorious cheesecakes *B*

SONG (1)

Variations in the text printed by Mitford and subsequent editors :

1. With beauty, with pleasure surrounded, to languish

2. And droop] To weep   source] cause

3. look] wish   4. Yet] To   6. Sounds] Words

SONG (2)

*Mason added to his transcript variants in ll. 9, 10, 12 which he
noted as* First Expressions; *these and variants in Walpole's letter
and in Mitford's MS. are given below :*

7. green] bloom *Mitford MS., with* green *in margin.*

8. such] this *Walpole*

9. Western] Warmer '*First Expression*': *so Mitford, with*
Western *in margin.*

10. Prove not always] Cannot prove that '*First Expression*';
Speak not always *Walpole*; *Mitford records a variant* Can ye prove.

12. Spare the honour] Dare not to reproach '*First Expression*':
Mitford gives this as a variant.

SATIRE ON THE HEADS OF HOUSES.

Variants in the Mitford copies :

2. I've pen'd] I penn'd   3. thy] the
6. hugely] largely   12. him] these
13. As *om.*   15. So *om.* 20. his] a
25. But *om.*   28. the] a
29. Pembroke] Pembroke   30. system] system

TOPHET.

Variations in the etching and in the version printed in the Gentleman's Magazine.

1, 2. *Etching:*

> Such Tophet was—so grind the bawling Fiend
> While frighted Prelates bow'd and call'd him Friend.

G.M.:

> Thus Tophet look'd ; so grinned the brawling fiend
> While frighted prelates bow'd and called him friend.

3, 4. *Omitted in the etching and in G.M.*

4. servile] civil *is written below as an alternative in the Pembroke transcript.*

LINES SPOKEN BY THE GHOST OF
JOHN DENNIS.

18. Stairs] *A piece of the letter is cut out : Walpole supplied the missing word.*

41. Orozmades] *So spelt by Gray, Walpole, and West.*

APPENDIX I.

STANZA'S WROTE IN A COUNTRY CHURCH-YARD.

[Printed from the original MS. now preserved in the Memorial Buildings of Eton College. Mitford's collations of this version are recorded in B.M. Add. MSS. 32561, ff. 180–1, and 32562, ff. 32–3.]

THE Curfeu tolls the Knell of parting Day,
The lowing Herd wind slowly o'er the Lea,
The Plowman homeward plods his weary Way,
And leaves the World to Darkness & to me.

Now fades the glimm'ring Landscape on the Sight,
And now the Air a solemn Stillness holds ;
Save, where the Beetle wheels his droning Flight,
Or drowsy Tinklings lull the distant Folds.

Save, that from yonder ivy-mantled Tower
The mopeing Owl does to the Moon complain
Of such as wandring [1] near her secret Bower
Molest her ancient [2] solitary Reign.

Beneath those rugged Elms, that Yewtree's Shade,
Where heaves the Turf in many a mould'ring Heap,
Each in his narrow Cell for ever laid
The rude Forefathers of the Hamlet [3] sleep.

---

[1] stray too *is written above* wandring.
[2] & pry into *is written above* Molest her ancient.
[3] Village *has been struck out and* Hamlet *written above.*

For ever sleep, the breezy Call of Morn,
Or Swallow twitt'ring from the strawbuilt Shed,
Or Chaunticleer so shrill or ecchoing Horn,
No more shall rouse them from their lowly Bed.

For them no more the blazeing Hearth shall burn,
Or busy Huswife ply her Evening Care ;
No Children run to lisp their Sire's Return,
Nor climb his Knees the coming [1] Kiss to share.

Oft did the Harvest to their Sickle yield ;
Their Furrow oft the stubborn Glebe has broke ;
How jocund did they drive their Team a-field !
How bow'd the Woods beneath their sturdy Stroke !

Let not Ambition mock their useful [2] Toil,
Their rustic Joys & Destiny obscure :
Nor Grandeur hear with a disdainful Smile
The short & simple Annals of the Poor.

The Boast of Heraldry the Pomp of Power,
And all, that Beauty, all that Wealth, e'er gave
Awaits alike th' inevitable Hour.
The Paths of Glory lead but to the Grave.

Forgive, ye Proud, th' involuntary Fault,
If Memory to these no Trophies raise,
Where thro' the long-drawn Ile, & fretted Vault
The pealing Anthem swells the Note of Praise.

Can storied Urn, or animated Bust,
Back to its Mansion call the fleeting Breath ?
Can Honour's voice awake [3] the silent dust,
Or Flattery sooth the dull cold Ear of Death ?

[1] envied *is written above and* doubtful? *is written in margin.*
[2] homely *is substituted for* useful *in margin.*
[3] provoke *is substituted for* awake *in margin.*

1. Perhaps in this neglected Spot is laid
   Some Heart, once pregnant with celestial Fire,
   Hands, that the Reins of Empire might have sway'd,
   Or waked to Ecstasy the living Lyre :

4.   Some Village Cato   [1] with dauntless Breast
   The little Tyrant of his Fields withstood ;
   Some mute inglorious Tully here may rest ;
   Some Caesar, guiltless of his Country's Blood.

2.   But Knowledge to their eyes her ample Page,
   Rich with the Spoils of Time, did ne'er unroll :
   Chill Penury had damp'd [2] their noble Rage,
   And froze the genial Current of the Soul.

3. Full many a Gem of purest Ray serene
   The dark unfathom'd Caves of Ocean bear.
   Full many a Flower is born to blush unseen
   And wast its Sweetness on the desert Air.

   Th' Applause of listening Senates to command,
   The Threats of Pain & Ruin to despise,
   To scatter Plenty o'er a smiling Land
   And read their Hist'ry in a Nation's Eyes,

   Their Fate [3] forbad : nor circumscribed alone
   Their struggling [4] Virtues, but their Crimes confined ;
   Forbad to wade thro' Slaughter to a Throne,
   And shut the Gates of Mercy on Mankind

[1] *A word is lost through the fraying of the paper at a crease.*
[2] depress'd repress'd *written above.*
[3] Lot *written above.*
[4] growing *written above.*

The struggleing Pangs of conscious Truth to hide,
To quench the Blushes of ingenuous Shame,
And at [1] the Shrine of Luxury & Pride
With [2] Incense hallowd in [3] the Muse's Flame.

The thoughtless World to Majesty may bow
Exalt the brave, & idolize Success
But more to Innocence their Safety owe
Than Power & Genius e'er conspired to bless

And thou, who mindful of the unhonour'd Dead
Dost in these Notes their [4] artless Tale relate
By Night & lonely Contemplation led
To linger in the gloomy Walks of Fate

Hark how the sacred Calm, that broods around
Bids ev'ry fierce tumultuous Passion cease
In still small Accents whisp'ring from the Ground
A grateful Earnest of eternal Peace

No more with Reason & thyself at Strife ;
Give anxious Cares & endless Wishes room
But thro' the cool sequester'd Vale of Life
Pursue the silent Tenour of thy Doom.

Far from the madding Crowd's ignoble Strife,
Their sober Wishes never knew to stray :
Along the cool sequester'd Vale of Life
They kept the silent [5] Tenour of their Way.

[1] Crown *written above* at.
[2] Burn *is struck out and* With *inserted above.*
[3] kindled at *written below,* by *instead of* in *written above.*
[4] *In* thy *the* y *is struck out and* eir *written above.*
[5] noiseless *written above.*

Yet even these Bones from Insult to protect
Some frail Memorial still erected nigh
With[1] uncouth Rhime, & shapeless Sculpture deckt
Implores the passing Tribute of a Sigh.

Their Name, their Years, spelt by th' unletter'd Muse
The Place of Fame, & Epitaph supply
And many a holy Text around she strews,
That teach the rustic Moralist to die.

For who to dumb Forgetfulness, a Prey,
This pleasing anxious Being e'er resign'd ;
Left the warm Precincts of the chearful Day,
Nor cast one longing lingring Look behind ?

On some fond Breast the parting Soul relies,
Some pious Drops the closing Eye requires :
Even from the Tomb the Voice of Nature cries,
And buried Ashes glow with Social Fires.

For Thee, who mindful &c: as above.

If chance that e'er some pensive Spirit more,
By sympathetic Musings here delay'd,
With vain, tho' kind, Enquiry shall explore
Thy once-loved Haunt, this long-deserted Shade.

Haply some hoary headed Swain shall say,
Oft have we seen him at the Peep of Dawn
With hasty Footsteps brush the Dews away
On the high Brow of yonder hanging Lawn

Him have we seen the Green-wood Side along
While o'er the Heath we hied, our Labours done,
Oft as the Woodlark piped her farewell Song
With whistful Eyes pursue the setting Sun.

---

[1] With *substituted for another word, perhaps* In, *which has been inked out.*

Oft at the Foot of yonder hoary [1] Beech
That wreathes its old fantastic Roots so high
His listless Length at Noontide would he stretch,
And pore upon the Brook that babbles by.

With Gestures quaint now smileing as in Scorn,
Mutt'ring his fond Conceits [2] he would he [3] rove,
Now drooping, woeful wan, [4] as one forlorn,
Or crazed with Care, or cross'd in hopeless Love.

One Morn we miss'd him on th' customd [5] Hill,
By [6] the Heath [7] and at [8] his fav'rite Tree.
Another came, nor yet beside the Rill,
Nor up the Lawn, nor at [8] the Wood was he.

[10] The next with Dirges meet in sad Array
Slow thro [11] the Church-way Path we saw him born
Approach & read, for thou can'st read the Lay
Wrote [12] on the Stone beneath that [13] ancient Thorn:

[1] spreading *is written above*, nodding *in the margin.*

[2] wayward fancies *is written above.*

[3] wont to *is struck out*, loved *is written above and struck out, finally* would he *is written above.*

[4] *The line originally stood* Now woeful wan, he droop'd. drooping *is inserted above and* he droop'd *is struck out.*

[5] ac[customd] ac *struck out.*

[6] Along *written above.*

[7] side *is written after* Heath *and struck out.*

[8] Near *written above* at.

[9] By *written above.*

[10] *Between these stanzas is written and struck out* There scatter'd oft, the earliest.

[11] By *written above.*

[12] Graved carved *written above.*

[13] yon *written above.*

There scatter'd oft the earliest of ye Year [1]
By Hands unseen are frequent [2] Vi'lets found
The Robin [3] loves to build & warble there
And little Footsteps lightly print the Ground.

Here [4] rests his Head upon the Lap of Earth
A Youth to Fortune & to Fame unknown
Fair Science frown'd not on his humble birth
And Melancholy mark'd him for her own

Large was his Bounty & his Heart sincere ;
Heaven did a Recompence as largely send.
He gave to Mis'ry all he had, a Tear.
He gained from Heav'n ; twas all he wish'd, a Friend

No further seek his Merits to disclose,
Nor seek [5] to draw them from their dread Abode
(His frailties there in trembling Hope repose)
The Bosom of his Father & his God.

[1] Spring *struck out and* year *written above.*

[2] Showers of *written above.*

[3] Redbreast *written above.*

[4] The Epitaph *is written along the outer margin at right angles to the* other stanzas.

[5] think *is written above* seek.

APPENDIX II.

GRAY'S REMOVAL FROM PETERHOUSE TO PEMBROKE HALL.

In March 1756 occurred ' the era ' in Gray's life. He moved from Peterhouse to Pembroke Hall. The facts relating to this sudden departure have been much disputed. Gray describes the event in a letter to Wharton of March 25, 1756.

' this may be look'd upon as a sort of Æra in a life so barren of events as mine, yet I shall treat it in Voltaire's manner, & only tell you, that I left my lodgings, because the rooms were noisy, & the People of the house dirty. this is all I would chuse to have said about it ; but if you in private should be curious enough to enter into a particular detail of facts & minute circumstances, Stonhewer who was witness to them will probably satisfy you.'

It is clear that Gray is keeping something back, something that was not much to his credit, and as he was of a very sensitive nature, he wished it to remain a secret. Stonhewer, the only witness, never divulged the truth. Sir Edmund Gosse gives a bold and picturesque description of the famous scene :

' The noisy fellow-commoners determined to have a lark at the timid little poet's expense, and one night in February, 1756, when Gray was asleep in bed, they suddenly alarmed him with a cry of fire on his staircase, having previously placed a tub of water under his window. The ruse succeeded only too well : Gray, without staying to put on his clothes, hooked his rope-ladder to the iron bar, and descended nimbly into the tub of water, from which he was rescued with shouts of laughter by the unmannerly youths. But the jest might easily have proved fatal ; as it was, he shivered in the February air so excessively that he had to be wrapped in the coat of a passing watchman, and to be carried into the college by the friendly Stonehewer.'

The story was told in some detail by Archibald Campbell in his *Sale of Authors*, which appeared in 1767. It takes the form of a dialogue between Apollo and Mercury :

' *Mercury*. You, waiter, bring out the poet in the watchman's coat, and set him on the table. . . .

' *Apollo*. I see this good company are not a little surprised, that so eminent a poet is wrapt up in a watchman's coat. Pray, Mercury, inform them how it happened. . . .

' *Mercury*. You must know, having made many unsuccessful attempts to catch this great poet, I was at last obliged to have recourse to stratagem. Though he has a great deal of poetical fire, nobody indeed more, yet is he extremely afraid of culinary fire, and keeps constantly by him a ladder of ropes to guard against all accidents of that sort. Knowing this, I hired some watchmen to raise the alarm of fire below his windows. Immediately the windows were seen to open, and the Poet descending in his shirt by his ladder. Thus we caught him at last, and one of the watchmen, to prevent his nerves being totally benumbed by frigorific torpor, lent him his great coat. . . .'

The author, however, refused to vouch for the truth of his facts. The account is interesting as showing that the story was current during the poet's lifetime. But we cannot suppose that Campbell heard it from any of the Gray circle. Mason in his note to the letter we have quoted adds nothing material. He speaks of the riotous character of some ' young men of fortune ' and how Gray complained to the authorities, and, finding that they paid too little attention to his remonstrance, quitted the college. Perhaps he would have said more but for Horace Walpole's warning. The latter wrote to Mason on April 17, 1774 : ' In Gray's own letters there is enough to offend : your notes added will involve him in the quarrel ; every silly story will be revived. . . . I would omit every passage that hints at the cause of his removal from Peterhouse.' The reviewer of Mason's edition of Gray's works in the *Gentleman's Magazine* for June 1775 adds considerably to the story given in Mason's note. 'We have heard that Mr. Gray being fearful of fire, especially after that in Cornhill, these very young men were so wantonly inconsiderate (to say no worse), as to alarm him at Midnight with the cry of it, that they might see him descend (which he was preparing to do), perhaps " headlong " like his Welsh bard, by a ladder of ropes, with which he was always furnished.'

From Mitford we get the most valuable evidence—more so since much of it has been corroborated by the College books. His life of Gray was first printed in the Eton Edition of 1847. Mitford heard from ' Dr. Gretton, the Master of Magdalene [who was formerly of Peterhouse] that " the young men of fortune " were the late Lord Egmont [then Mr. Percival], a Mr. Forrester, a Mr. Williams, and others ; that Gray complained to the Master, Dr. Law, [afterwards] Bishop of Carlisle ; and he offended Gray by the little regard he paid to the complaint, and by his calling it " a boyish frolic ".'

From this confused mass of evidence we can piece together a tolerably true account of the episode. In 1748 Gray's house in Cornhill was burnt down. This was perhaps the beginning of that morbid terror of fire which seems to have strongly possessed him. As a precaution against fire, we know from a letter dated January 9, 1756, that he asked Wharton to buy for him ' a Rope-Ladder (for my Neighbours every day make a great progress in drunkenness, wch gives me reason to look about me). . . . I suppose it must have strong hooks, or something equivalent, a-top, to throw over an iron bar to be fix'd within-side of my window '. An iron bar in the rooms Gray occupied bears testimony to the fact that he carried out his intention. The suddenness of his departure arouses our suspicions. He was in residence during the week ending March 5, 1756. His

name was entered for the following week, and then struck
through by the Butler. The Pembroke admission book records
'Thomas Gray, LL.B., admissus est ex collegio Divi Petri.
March 6, 1756'. These entries fix the date of his migration.
Had there been nothing else besides noisy rooms and dirty
people to complain of, it would seem more natural to move
at the end of term. Mr. Tovey regards the whole story very
sceptically. But he is mistaken when he states that Law only
succeeded to the Mastership in the year 1756, and that Keene
(Bishop of Chester) was probably still acting as Master early
in the year. Keene actually resigned on October 25, 1754,
so that Law had been Master for more than a year when
Gray laid his complaint before him. The rest of Dr. Gretton's
story has now been largely confirmed by Dr. Walker from the
evidence of College records. Forrester and Bennet Williams
were, like Gretton, fellow Commoners, and in residence for the
week ending March 5, 1756. They actually dined in Gray's
company at High Table during that week. From the Bursar's
book Dr. Walker has discovered that George Forrester occupied
the set of rooms opposite to Gray and that Bennet Williams
had rooms on the ground floor of the same staircase. Lord
Egmont, who is mentioned as the other culprit, was never at
Peterhouse. But the part he played in it is confirmed by
a letter dated March 12, 1756, only six days after the event,
from the Rev. John Sharp, a fellow of Corpus Christi College,
Cambridge. The letter was quoted by Professor Kittredge of
Harvard in the New York *Nation* of September 12, 1900, from
Nichol's *Illustrations*, and is cited by Tovey in the Addenda
to his edition of Gray's letters (ii. 304).

'Mr Gray, our elegant Poet, and delicate Fellow Commoner
of Peter-house, has just removed to Pembroke-hall, in resentment of some usage he met with at the former place. The
case is much talked of, and is this. He is much afraid of fire
and was a great sufferer in Cornhill; he has ever since kept
a ladder of ropes by him, soft as the silky cords by which Romeo

ascended to his Juliet, and has had an iron machine fixed to his bed-room window. The other morning, Lord Percival and some Petrenchians, going a hunting, were determined to have a little sport before they set out, and thought it would be no bad diversion to make Gray bolt, as they called it, so ordered their man Joe Draper to roar out fire. A delicate white night-cap is said to have appeared at the window; but finding the mistake, retired again to the couch. The young fellows, had he descended, were determined, they said, to have whipped the butterfly up again.'

With this evidence the story becomes historical. Gray was afraid of fire, and obtained a rope ladder as a means of escape in case of an alarm. Lord Percival and certain fellow commoners of Peterhouse, among them George Forrester and Bennet Williams, knowing Gray's weakness, gave a false alarm, and Gray either descended or more probably prepared to descend from his window by his rope ladder. He complained to Dr. Law, failed to get his complaint attended to, and in consequence crossed Trumpington Street to take up his abode in the Hitcham Building of Pembroke Hall. The remainder of the story—the tub—the watchman's coat—have no other foundation than legend and the imaginative genius of Gray's biographer.

POEMS

OF

WILLIAM COLLINS

EDITED BY

CHRISTOPHER STONE

AND

AUSTIN LANE POOLE.

o

PREFACE TO THIRD EDITION.

The Poems of William Collins, edited by Mr. Christopher Stone (Frowde, London, 1907), forms the basis of this edition. The versions given in the text follow in most cases the first printed editions, but as Collins's punctuation does cause some grammatical difficulties, his later punctuation of the *Eclogues* has been adopted where it is useful. A few other slight changes of punctuation, and some editorial emendations, are recorded in the notes. The early Sonnet, ' When Phœbe formed a wanton smile ', is reprinted from the *Gentleman's Magazine* of October 1739, where it first appeared ; but the Song written about the same time, ' Young Damon of the Vale is dead ', was not printed in the poet's lifetime, and was not even included in the first collected edition of the poems by Langhorne in 1765. It is now printed from the *Gentleman's Magazine*, February 1788, where it appeared anonymously. (I am indebted for this reference as well as for other corrections, immediately to Mr. H. O. White (*Times* Literary Supplement, 5 April 1928), and ultimately to Professor A. D. McKillop (*Modern Language Notes*, Baltimore, 1923). *The Persian Eclogues* are printed from the first edition of 1742, except that the refrains repeated throughout the second and third eclogues are printed in full instead of the abbreviations, ' Sad was the Hour, &c.', ' Be every Youth, &c.' ; and two necessary corrections are adopted from a copy with Collins's autograph notes. These were given effect to in the second edition, which appeared in 1757 as *Oriental Eclogues*. The verses to Sir Thomas

Hanmer are reprinted from the original edition of 1743; but the second edition of 1744 varies so much from the first that I have printed it entire as an appendix. The *Odes on Several Descriptive and Allegorical Subjects* are reprinted from the only authoritative edition of 1747 where all were printed for the first time, with the single exception of the Ode addressed to Miss Elizabeth Goddard *On the Death of Colonel Ross*, which had already appeared in Dodsley's *Museum* in June 1746. The *Ode on the Death of Thomson* is printed from the original pamphlet published by Manby and Cox in 1749. *The Song from Shakespear's ' Cymbelyne '* is printed from *An Epistle : address to Sir Thomas Hanmer, &c.*, second edition, 1744. The *Ode on the Popular Superstitions of the Highlands of Scotland* was first printed in the *Transactions* of the Royal Society of Edinburgh in 1788 from a copy given by Collins to Mr. Home, to whom it was addressed. The one and a half stanzas written to supply a gap in the MS. are omitted, but rather than print Collins's own lines with gaps, Dr. Alexander Carlyle's suggestions are included between square brackets. The verses *Written on a paper which contained a piece of bride-cake* are taken from the *Gentleman's Magazine*, May 1765, where they first appeared. All the explanatory notes at the foot of the page were added by the poet himself.

For the List of Chief Editions of Collins's Works I am indebted to Mr. Stone, and for the revision of the second and third editions to Mr. Frederick Page, of the Oxford University Press. To Mr. Iolo A. Williams I am indebted for Appendix II. The third edition owes much to Professor H. W. Garrod's book on Collins (1928).

AUSTIN L. POOLE.

1936.

CONTENTS.

PLATES.

* From a copy kindly lent by the late H. Buxton Forman.

LIST OF THE CHIEF EDITIONS OF
THE WORKS OF COLLINS.

Persian Eclogues. London, Roberts, 1742 (see title-page, pp. 208, 209).

Verses humbly address'd to Sir Thomas Hanmer on his edition of Shakespear's Works, by a Gentleman of Oxford. London, Cooper, 1743 (see title-page, p. 231).

An Epistle : addrest to Sir Thomas Hanmer, on his Edition of Shakespear's Works. The Second Edition. To which is added, A Song from the *Cymbelyne* of the same Author. By Mr. William Collins, of Magdalene-College in Oxford. London : Dodsley and Cooper, 1744.

Odes on several Descriptive and Allegoric Subjects, by William Collins. London, Millar, 1747. The title-page (see p. 241) bears this date, but the Odes actually appeared in December 1746.

An Ode occasion'd by the death of Mr. Thomson, by William Collins. London, Manby, 1749 (see title-page, p. 289).

The Passions, an Ode. 4to. Winchester. N.D. [1750]. [This and the Oxford edition below have the last twenty-four lines rewritten by the Earl of Lichfield.]

The Passions, an Ode. Written by Mr. Collins. Set to Musick by Dr. Hayes. Performed at the Theatre in Oxford, July 2, 1750.

Oriental Eclogues. London, Payne, 1757 (anonymously).

The Poetical Calendar. Written and selected by Francis Fawkes, M.A., and William Woty. 1763. Vol. xi. For November contains (pp. 17–75) the four Oriental Eclogues, the Twelve Odes, the Epistle to Sir Thomas Hanmer, A Song from Shakespear's Cymbeline. Vol. xii. For December contains (pp. 104–6) the Ode on the Death of Mr. James Thomson.

The Poetical Works of Mr. William Collins, with Memoirs of the Author ; and Observations on his genius and writings, by J. Langhorne. London, Becket and Dehondt, 1765.

Poetical Works. Glasgow, Foulis, 1770, 1787.

An Ode on the Popular Superstitions of the Highlands of Scotland, etc. London, Bell, 1788.

    [The spurious edition. This Ode first appeared in the *Transactions* of the Royal Society of Edinburgh, 1788.]

Poetical Works, edited by Mrs. Barbauld. London, Cadell and Davies, 1794.

Poetical Works. Colchester, Keymer, 1796.

Poetical Works, enriched with elegant engravings. London, 1798.

Poetical Works (Langhorne's Commentary, Johnson's ' Life ' ; engravings from designs by Westall). London, Sharpe, 1804.

Poetical Works, edited by the Rev. Alexander Dyce. London, Pickering, 1827.

Poems, edited by W. Crowe. Bath, 1828.

Poems, with Memoir (by Sir Harris Nicolas), and Essay by Sir Egerton Brydges. (Aldine Poets.) London, Pickering, 1830.

Poems, with Memoir, by W. Moy Thomas. London, 1858.

Poems, edited by W. C. Bronson. London, Ginn & Co., 1898.

Poems, with Memoir, by Christopher Stone. London, Frowde, 1907.

Poems, edited with an Introductory Study by Edmund Blunden. The Haslewood Books, 1929.

CHRONOLOGICAL TABLE.

A.D.	ÆT.	
1703		William Collins, a hatter and twice Mayor of Chichester, married Elizabeth Martin. Their children were :
1704		(1) Elizabeth.
1705		(2) Anne.
1721		(3) William, the poet, born on Christmas Day at Chichester. [He probably received his early education at the Prebendal School, Chichester.]
1733	11	Admitted as a scholar at Winchester College, under Dr. John Burton (January 19). Became the friend of Joseph Warton.
1734	12	Composed his first poem, *The Battle of the Schoolbooks*. One line alone survives : ' And every Gradus flapp'd his leathern wing.' William Collins, senior, died Dec. 31.
1739	17	His *Sonnet*, ' When Phœbe form'd a wanton smile ', published in the *Gentleman's Magazine*, October. While still at school he wrote the *Song* ' Young Damon of the Vale is dead ' and also began his *Persian Eclogues*.
1740	18	Appeared first on the list of scholars at New College ; but as no vacancy occurred, went as a Commoner to Queen's College, Oxford (March 21).
1741	19	Elected to a Demyship at Magdalen (July 29), possibly through the influence of his cousin, William Payne, who was then a Fellow. Among his friends at Oxford was Gilbert White, who, with Joseph Warton, was at Oriel.
1742	20	*Persian Eclogues* published (January).
1743	21	Graduated as B.A. (November 18). The *Verses to Sir Thomas Hanmer* published, as by ' a Gentleman of Oxford '.

A.D.	ÆT.	
1744	22	On failing to obtain a Fellowship he left Oxford, where his creditors were growing insistent, and went to London. July 13 his mother died, leaving him a small property, which he quickly dissipated. *An Epistle : addrest to Sir Thomas Hanmer*, second edition, with Collins's name, with the *Song from 'Cymbelyne'* published.
1745	23	In the summer Collins visited his uncle, Colonel Martin of the 8th Regiment of Foot, quartered in Flanders. The Colonel thought him ' too indolent even for the Army ' and recommended him to take Holy Orders. He applied to Mr. Green, Rector of Birdham, near Chichester, for a curacy, but was dissuaded from entering the Church by a tobacconist in Fleet Street. Lodging with a Miss Bundy in Soho on an allowance from his cousin, George Payne, he entered on a literary career. In London he formed a close friendship with James Thomson, the poet, and with John Ragsdale, a neighbour of Thomson's at Richmond. He was also introduced into a circle of actors—among them Foote, Garrick, and Quin—and about this time (or in 1747) made the acquaintance of Dr. Johnson.
1746	24	Collins goes to Flanders a second time. The *Odes on Several Descriptive and Allegorical Subjects* were published (December) : 1000 copies.
1747	25	Sells his father's house at Chichester. Projected (1) a Commentary on Aristotle's *Poetics*, (2) The Friendly Examiner, or Letters of Polémon and Philéthus, (3) The Clarendon Review ; also undertook to write memoirs for the *Biographia Britannica*. Colonel Martin, being wounded in the Battle of Val in Flanders, returned to live with his nieces at Chiches-

A.D.	ÆT.	
		ter. ?Anne Collins married Captain Hugh Sempill.
1748	26	James Thomson died (August).
1749	27	Colonel Martin died, leaving to Collins about £2,000, whereon Collins abandoned his projected Commentary on the *Poetics*, and bought up and destroyed the remainder of *Odes*, 1746. Collins composed the *Ode on the Death of Thomson* (published in June). At Winchester met John Home, to whom he addressed his *Ode on the Popular Superstitions of the Highlands* that same year.
1750	28	*The Passions* set to music and performed at Oxford (2 July). Elizabeth Collins married Lieutenant Nathaniel Tanner (November).
1751	29	Collins fell dangerously ill, recovered, but was ever after subject to melancholia. Travelled in France and afterwards visited Bath in the hope of ridding himself of his depression by change of scenery. Johnson visited him at Islington.
1754	32	Visited Oxford for a month in the summer, where he lodged opposite Christ Church. Here he saw much of Thomas Warton, then a Fellow of Trinity. His melancholia became rapidly worse, and he was removed for a short time to McDonald's Madhouse in Chelsea. Thence he returned to Chichester, where he lived till his death, with Mrs. Sempill. Elizabeth Tanner died.
1756	34	J. Warton inserts one of Collins's fragments in his *Essay on Pope*. Johnson enquires after him (April 15). ' I wrote him a letter which he never answered.'
1757	35	The *Persian Eclogues* reissued (anonymously, with some corrections) as *Oriental Eclogues*.
1759	37	William Collins died, June 12, and was buried in St. Andrew's Church, Chichester.

POEMS.

SONNET.

[Written 1739: first published over the signature 'Delicatulus' in the *Gentleman's Magazine*, October 1739.]

WHEN *Phœbe* form'd a wanton smile,
    My soul ! it reach'd not here !
Strange, that thy peace, thou trembler, flies
    Before a rising tear !

From midst the drops, my love is born,
    That o'er those eyelids rove :
Thus issued from a teeming wave
    The fabled queen of love.

PERSIAN

ECLOGUES.

Written originally for the

ENTERTAINMENT

OF THE

Ladies of *TAURIS*.

And now first translated, &c.

Illos primos capis, Oreas afflavit, anhelis. — Virg.

Quod si non hic tantas fructus ostenderetur,
& si ex his studiis delectatio sola pete-
retur; tamen, ut opinor, hanc animi
remissionem humanissimam ac liberalissi-
mam judicaretis.
                    Cic. pro Arch. Poeta.

LONDON:

Printed for J. ROBERTS in *Warwick-Lane* 1742.

(Price Six-pence.)

By Mr Collins (Written at School)

Winchester

PERSIAN

ECLOGUES.

Written originally for the

ENTERTAINMENT

OF THE

Ladies of *TAURIS*.

And now first translated, *&c.*

---

*Quod si non hìc tantas fructus ostenderetur,
& si ex his studiis delectatis sola pete-
retur ; tamen, ut opinor, hanc animi
remissionem humanissimam ac liberalissi-
mam judicaretis.*

Cic. pro Arch. Poeta.

LONDON:

Printed for J. ROBERTS, in *Warwick-Lane.* 1742.

(Price Six-pence.)

THE

PREFACE.

It is with the Writings of Mankind, in some Measure, as with their Complexions or their Dress; each Nation hath a Peculiarity in all these, to distinguish it from the rest of the World.

The Gravity of the *Spaniard*, and the Levity of the *Frenchman*, are as evident in all their Productions as in their Persons themselves; and the Stile of my Countrymen is as naturally Strong and Nervous, as that of an *Arabian* or *Persian* is rich and figurative.

There is an Elegancy and Wildness of Thought which recommends all their Compositions; and our Genius's are as much too cold for the Entertainment of such Sentiments, as our Climate is for their Fruits and Spices. If any of these Beauties are to be found in the following *Eclogues*, I hope my Reader will consider them as an Argument of their being Original. I received them at the Hands of a Merchant, who had made it his Business to enrich himself with the Learning, as well as the Silks and Carpets of the *Persians*. The little Information I could gather concerning their Author, was, That his Name was *Mahamed*, and that he was a Native of *Tauris*.

It was in that City that he died of a Distemper fatal in those Parts, whilst he was engag'd in celebrating the Victories of his favourite Monarch, *the Great Abbas*. As to the *Eclogues* themselves, they give a very just View of the Miseries and Inconveniencies, as well as the Felicities, that attend one of the finest Countries in the East.

The Time of the Writing them was probably in the Beginning of *Sha Sultan Hosseyn*'s Reign, the Successor of *Sefi* or *Solyman* the Second.

Whatever Defects, as, I doubt not, there will be many, fall under the Reader's Observation, I hope his Candour will incline him to make the following Reflections :

That the Works of *Orientals* contain many Peculiarities, and that thro' Defect of Language few *European* Translators can do them Justice.

E C L O G U E the FIRST.

SELIM; *or, the Shepherd's Moral.*

SCENE, *a Valley near* Bagdat.

TIME, *the* MORNING.

YE *Persian* Maids, attend your Poet's Lays,
And hear how Shepherds pass their golden Days:
Not all are blest, whom Fortune's Hand sustains
With Wealth in Courts, nor all that haunt the Plains:
Well may your Hearts believe the Truths I tell;
'Tis Virtue makes the Bliss, where'er we dwell.

Thus *Selim* sung, by sacred Truth inspir'd;
No Praise the Youth, but her's alone desir'd:
Wise in himself, his meaning Songs convey'd
Informing Morals to the Shepherd Maid;   10
Or taught the Swains that surest Bliss to find,
What Groves nor Streams bestow, a virtuous Mind.

When sweet and od'rous, like an Eastern Bride,
The radiant Morn resum'd her orient Pride,

When wanton Gales along the Valleys play,
Breathe on each Flow'r, and bear their Sweets away;
By *Tigris'* wand'ring waves he sate, and sung
This useful Lesson for the Fair and Young.

  Ye *Persian* Dames, he said, to ye belong,
Well may they please, the Morals of my Song :   20
No fairer Maids, I trust, than ye are found,
Grac'd with soft Arts, the peopled World around !
The Morn that lights you, to your Loves supplies
Each gentler Ray delicious to your Eyes :
For ye those Flow'rs her fragrant Hands bestow,
And yours the Love that Kings delight to know.
Yet think not these, all beauteous as they are,
The best kind Blessings Heav'n can grant the Fair !
Who trust alone in Beauty's feeble Ray,
* *Balsord*'s Pearls have more of Worth than they ;   30
Drawn from the Deep, they sparkle to the Sight,
And all-unconscious shoot a lust'rous Light :
Such are the Maids, and such the Charms they boast,
By Sense unaided, or to Virtue lost.
Self-flattering Sex ! your Hearts believe in vain
That Love shall blind, when once he fires the Swain ;

---

 * The Gulph of that Name, famous for the Pearl-fishery.

Or hope a Lover by your Faults to win,
As Spots on Ermin beautify the Skin :
Who seeks secure to rule, be first her Care
Each softer Virtue that adorns the Fair,   40
Each tender Passion Man delights to find,
The lov'd Perfections of a female Mind.

Blest were the Days, when Wisdom held her Reign,
And Shepherds sought her on the silent Plain,
With Truth she wedded in the secret Grove,
The fair-eyed Truth, and Daughters bless'd their Love.

O haste, fair Maids ! ye Virtues come away,
Sweet Peace and Plenty lead you on your way !
The balmy Shrub, for ye, shall love our Shore,
By *Ind'* excell'd or *Araby* no more.   50

Lost to our Fields, for so the Fates ordain,
The dear Deserters shall return again.
O come, thou Modesty, as they decree,
The Rose may then improve her Blush by Thee.
Here make thy Court amidst our rural Scene,
And Shepherd-Girls shall own Thee for their Queen.

With Thee be Chastity, of all afraid,

Distrusting all, a wise suspicious Maid ;

But Man the most—not more the Mountain Doe

Holds the swift Falcon for her deadly Foe.   60

Cold is her Breast, like Flow'rs that drink the Dew ;

A silken Veil conceals her from the View.

No wild Desires amidst thy Train be known,

But Faith, whose Heart is fix'd on one alone :

Desponding Meekness with her down-cast Eyes,

And friendly Pity full of tender Sighs ;

And Love the last : By these your Hearts approve,

These are the Virtues that must lead to Love.

   Thus sung the Swain ; and Eastern Legends say,

The maids of *Bagdat* verify'd the Lay :   70

Dear to the Plains, the Virtues came along,

The Shepherds lov'd, and *Selim* bless'd his Song.

The END of the First ECLOGUE.

E C L O G U E the SECOND.

HASSAN; *or, the Camel-driver.*

SCENE, *the Desert.*

TIME, MID-DAY.

In silent Horror o'er the Desart-Waste
The Driver *Hassan* with his Camels past.
One Cruise of Water on his Back he bore,
And his light Scrip contain'd a scanty Store:
A Fan of painted Feathers in his Hand,
To guard his shaded Face from scorching Sand.
The sultry Sun had gain'd the middle Sky,
And not a Tree, and not an Herb was nigh.
The Beasts, with Pain, their dusty Way pursue,
Shrill roar'd the Winds, and dreary was the View!   10
With desp'rate Sorrow wild, th' affrighted Man
Thrice sigh'd, thrice strook his Breast, and thus began:
  Sad was the Hour, and luckless was the Day,
  When first from Schiraz' *Walls I bent my Way.*

Ah ! little thought I of the blasting Wind,
The Thirst or pinching Hunger that I find !
Bethink thee, *Hassan*, where shall Thirst assuage,
When fails this Cruise, his unrelenting Rage ?
Soon shall this Scrip its precious Load resign ;
Then what but Tears and Hunger shall be thine ?   20

Ye mute Companions of my Toils, that bear
In all my Griefs a more than equal Share !
Here, where no Springs in Murmurs break away,
Or Moss-crown'd Fountains mitigate the Day,
In vain ye hope the green Delights to know,
Which Plains more blest, or verdant Vales bestow :
Here Rocks alone, and tasteless Sands are found,
And faint and sickly Winds for ever howl around.
Sad was the Hour, and luckless was the Day,
When first from Schiraz' *Walls I bent my Way !*   30

Curst be the Gold and Silver which persuade
Weak Men to follow far-fatiguing Trade !
The Lilly-Peace outshines the silver Store,
And Life is dearer than the golden Ore.
Yet Money tempts us o'er the Desart brown,
To ev'ry distant Mart, and wealthy Town :

Full oft we tempt the Land, and oft the Sea ;
And are we only yet repay'd by Thee ?
Ah ! why was Ruin so attractive made,
Or why fond Man so easily betray'd ?   40
Why heed we not, whilst mad we haste along,
The gentle Voice of Peace, or Pleasure's Song ?
Or wherefore think the flow'ry Mountain's Side,
The Fountain's Murmurs, and the Valley's Pride,
Why think we these less pleasing to behold,
Than dreary Desarts, if they lead to Gold ?
    Sad was the Hour, and luckless was the Day,
    When first from Schiraz' *Walls I bent my Way!*

    O cease, my Fears ! all frantic as I go,
When Thought creates unnumber'd Scenes of Woe,   50
What if the Lion in his Rage I meet !
Oft in the Dust I view his printed Feet :
And fearful ! oft, when Day's declining Light
Yields her pale Empire to the Mourner Night,
By Hunger rous'd, he scours the groaning Plain,
Gaunt Wolves and sullen Tygers in his Train :
Before them Death with Shrieks directs their Way,
Fills the wild Yell, and leads them to their Prey.
    Sad was the Hour, and luckless was the Day,
    When first from Schiraz' *Walls I bent my Way!*   60

At that dead Hour the silent Asp shall creep,
If ought of rest I find, upon my Sleep :
Or some swoln Serpent twist his Scales around,
And wake to Anguish with a burning Wound.
Thrice happy they, the wise contented Poor,
From Lust of Wealth, and Dread of Death secure !
They tempt no Desarts, and no Griefs they find ;
Peace rules the Day, where Reason rules the Mind.
 Sad was the Hour, and luckless was the Day,
 When first from Schiraz' *Walls I bent my Way!* 70

O hapless Youth ! for she thy Love hath won,
The tender *Zara*, will be most undone !
Big swell'd my Heart, and own'd the pow'rful Maid,
When fast she dropt her Tears, as thus she said :
" Farewel the Youth whom Sighs could not detain,
" Whom *Zara*'s breaking Heart implor'd in vain ;
" Yet as thou go'st, may ev'ry Blast arise,
" Weak and unfelt as these rejected Sighs !
" Safe o'er the Wild, no Perils mayst thou see,
" No Griefs endure, nor weep, false Youth, like me." 80
O let me safely to the Fair return,
Say with a Kiss, she must not, shall not mourn.

Go teach my Heart to lose its painful Fears,
Recall'd by Wisdom's Voice, and *Zara*'s Tears.

He said, and call'd on Heav'n to bless the Day,
When back to *Schiraz*' Walls he bent his Way.

The END of the Second ECLOGUE.

E C L O G U E the T H I R D.

ABRA ; *or*, *the* Georgian *Sultana.*

SCENE, *a Forest.*

TIME, *the* EVENING.

IN *Georgia*'s Land, where *Teflis'* Tow'rs are seen,
In distant View along the level Green,
While Ev'ning Dews enrich the glitt'ring Glade,
And the tall Forests cast a longer Shade,
Amidst the Maids of *Zagen*'s peaceful Grove,
Emyra sung the pleasing Cares of Love.

Of *Abra* first began the tender Strain,
Who led her Youth with Flocks upon the Plain:
At Morn she came those willing Flocks to lead,
Where Lillies rear them in the wat'ry Mead ;   10
From early Dawn the live-long Hours she told,
'Till late at silent Eve she penn'd the Fold.
Deep in the Grove beneath the secret Shade,
A various Wreath of od'rous Flow'rs she made :

* Gay-motley'd Pinks and sweet Junquils she chose,
The Violet-blue that on the Moss-bank grows ;
All-sweet to Sense, the flaunting Rose was there ;
The finish'd Chaplet well-adorn'd her Hair.

Great *Abbas* chanc'd that fated Morn to stray,
By Love conducted from the Chace away ;   20
Among the vocal Vales he heard her Song,
And sought the Vales and echoing Groves among :
At length he found, and woo'd the rural Maid ;
She knew the Monarch, and with Fear obey'd.
  Be ev'ry Youth like Royal Abbas *mov'd,*
  And ev'ry Georgian *Maid like* Abra *lov'd !*

The Royal Lover bore her from the Plain ;
Yet still her Crook and bleating Flock remain :
Oft as she went, she backward turn'd her View,
And bad that Crook and bleating Flock Adieu.   30
Fair happy Maid ! to other Scenes remove,
To richer Scenes of golden Pow'r and Love !
Go leave the simple Pipe, and Shepherd's Strain ;
With Love delight thee, and with *Abbas* reign.
  Be ev'ry Youth like Royal Abbas *mov'd,*
  And ev'ry Georgian *Maid like* Abra *lov'd !*

  * That these Flowers are found in very great Abundance in some
of the Provinces of *Persia*; see the *Modern History* of the ingenious
Mr. *Salmon*.

Yet midst the Blaze of Courts she fix'd her Love,
On the cool Fountain, or the shady Grove ;
Still with the Shepherd's Innocence her Mind
To the sweet Vale, and flow'ry Mead inclin'd ;   40
And oft as Spring renew'd the Plains with Flow'rs,
Breath'd his soft Gales, and led the fragrant Hours,
With sure Return she sought the sylvan Scene,
The breezy Mountains, and the Forests green.
Her Maids around her mov'd, a duteous Band !
Each bore a Crook all-rural in her Hand :
Some simple Lay, of Flocks and Herds they sung ;
With Joy the Mountain, and the Forest rung.
  Be ev'ry Youth like Royal Abbas *mov'd,*
  And ev'ry Georgian *Maid like* Abra *lov'd !*   50

And oft the Royal Lover left the Care,
And Thorns of State, attendant on the Fair :
Oft to the Shades and low-roof'd Cots retir'd,
Or sought the Vale where first his Heart was fir'd ;
A Russet Mantle, like a Swain, he wore,
And thought of Crowns and busy Courts no more.
  Be ev'ry Youth like Royal Abbas *mov'd,*
  And ev'ry Georgian *Maid like* Abra *lov'd !*

Blest was the Life, that Royal *Abbas* led :
Sweet was his Love, and innocent his Bed.   60
What if in Wealth the noble Maid excel ;
The simple Shepherd Girl can love as well.
Let those who rule on *Persia*'s jewell'd Throne,
Be fam'd for Love, and gentlest Love alone :
Or wreath, like *Abbas*, full of fair Renown,
The Lover's Myrtle, with the Warrior's Crown.

Oh happy Days ! the Maids around her say ;
Oh haste, profuse of Blessings, haste away !
  Be ev'ry Youth, like Royal Abbas, *mov'd* ;
  And ev'ry Georgian *Maid, like* Abra, *lov'd !*   70

The END of the Third ECLOGUE.

ECLOGUE the FOURTH.

AGIB *and* SECANDER ; *or, the Fugitives.*

SCENE, *a Mountain in* Circassia.

TIME, MIDNIGHT.

In fair *Circassia*, where, to Love inclin'd,
Each Swain was blest, for ev'ry Maid was kind ;
At that still Hour, when awful Midnight reigns,
And none, but Wretches, haunt the twilight Plains ;
What Time the Moon had hung her Lamp on high,
And past in Radiance, thro' the cloudless Sky :
Sad o'er the Dews, two Brother Shepherds fled,
Where wild'ring Fear and desp'rate Sorrow led.
Fast as they prest their Flight, behind them lay
Wide ravag'd Plains, and Valleys stole away.   10
Along the Mountain's bending Sides they ran,
Till faint and weak *Secander* thus began.

Secander.

O stay thee, *Agib*, for my Feet deny,
No longer friendly to my Life, to fly.
Friend of my Heart, O turn thee and survey,
Trace our sad Flight thro' all its length of Way !
And first review that long-extended Plain,
And yon wide Groves, already past with Pain !
Yon ragged Cliff, whose dang'rous Path we try'd !
And last this lofty Mountain's weary Side !   20

Agib.

Weak as thou art, yet hapless must thou know
The Toils of Flight, or some severer Woe !
Still as I haste, the *Tartar* shouts behind,
And Shrieks and Sorrows load the sad'ning Wind :
In rage of Heart, with Ruin in his Hand,
He blasts our Harvests, and deforms our Land.
Yon Citron Grove, whence first in Fear we came,
Droops its fair Honours to the conqu'ring Flame :
Far fly the Swains, like us, in deep Despair,
And leave to ruffian Bands their fleecy Care.   30

Secander.

Unhappy Land, whose Blessings tempt the Sword,
In vain, unheard, thou call'st thy *Persian* Lord !
In vain thou court'st him, helpless to thine Aid,
To shield the Shepherd, and protect the Maid !
Far off in thoughtless Indolence resign'd,
Soft Dreams of Love and Pleasure sooth his Mind :
'Midst fair *Sultanas* lost in idle Joy,
No Wars alarm him, and no Fears annoy.

Agib.

Yet these green Hills, in Summer's sultry Heat,
Have lent the Monarch oft a cool Retreat.   40
Sweet to the Sight is *Zabran*'s flow'ry Plain,
And once by Maids and Shepherds lov'd in vain !
No more the Virgins shall delight to rove,
By *Sargis*' Banks, or *Irwan*'s shady Grove :
On *Tarkie*'s Mountain catch the cooling Gale,
Or breathe the Sweets of *Aly*'s flow'ry Vale :
Fair Scenes ! but, ah ! no more with Peace possest,
With Ease alluring, and with Plenty blest.
No more the Shepherds' whit'ning Seats appear,
Nor the kind Products of a bounteous Year ;
No more the Date with snowy Blossoms crown'd,
But Ruin spreads her baleful Fires around.

Secander.

In vain *Circassia* boasts her spicy Groves,
For ever fam'd for pure and happy Loves :
In vain she boasts her fairest of the Fair,
Their Eyes' blue languish, and their golden Hair !
Those Eyes in Tears their fruitless Grief must send;
Those Hairs the *Tartar*'s cruel Hand shall rend.

Agib.

Ye *Georgian* Swains that piteous learn from far
Circassia's Ruin, and the Waste of War :   60
Some weightier Arms than Crooks and Staves prepare,
To shield your Harvests, and defend your Fair :
The *Turk* and *Tartar* like Designs pursue,
Fix'd to destroy, and stedfast to undo.
Wild as his Land, in native Deserts bred,
By Lust incited, or by Malice led,
The Villain-*Arab*, as he prowls for Prey,
Oft marks with Blood and wasting Flames the Way ;
Yet none so cruel as the *Tartar* Foe,
To Death inur'd, and nurst in Scenes of Woe.   70

Q

He said ; when loud along the Vale was heard
A shriller Shriek, and nearer Fires appear'd :
Th' affrighted Shepherds thro' the Dews of Night,
Wide o'er the Moon-light Hills, renew'd their Flight.

The END of the Fourth and last
ECLOGUE.

VERSES

Humbly Address'd

TO

Sir *THOMAS HANMER*.

On his EDITION of

Shakespear's WORKS.

By a GENTLEMAN *of* OXFORD.

LONDON:

Printed for M. COOPER, in *Pater-noster-Row.* 1743.

[Price Six Pence.]

To

SIR THOMAS HANMER.

SIR,

WHILE, own'd by You, with Smiles the Muse surveys
Th' expected Triumph of her sweetest Lays:
While, stretch'd at Ease, she boasts your Guardian Aid,
Secure, and happy in her sylvan Shade:
Excuse her Fears, who scarce a Verse bestows,
In just Remembrance of the Debt she owes;
With conscious Awe she hears the Critic's Fame,
And blushing hides her Wreath at *Shakespear*'s Name.

Long slighted *Fancy*, with a Mother's Care,
Wept o'er his Works, and felt the last Despair.   10
Torn from her Head, she saw the Roses fall,
By all deserted, tho' admir'd by all.
" And oh! she cry'd, shall Science still resign
" Whate'er is Nature's, and whate'er is mine?
" Shall *Taste* and *Art*, but shew a cold Regard,
" And scornful Pride reject th' unletter'd Bard?

" Ye myrtled Nymphs, who own my gentle Reign,

" Tune the sweet Lyre, and grace my airy Train !

" If, where ye rove, your searching Eyes have known

" One perfect Mind, which Judgment calls its own :　　20

" There ev'ry Breast its fondest Hopes must bend,

" And ev'ry Muse with Tears await her Friend.

'Twas then fair *Isis* from her Stream arose,

In kind Compassion of her Sister's Woes.

'Twas then she promis'd to the mourning Maid

Th' immortal Honours, which thy Hands have paid :

" My best-lov'd Son (she said) shall yet restore

" Thy ruin'd Sweets, and Fancy weep no more.

Each rising Art by slow Gradation moves,

Toil builds on Toil, and Age on Age improves.　　30

The Muse alone unequal dealt her Rage,

And grac'd with noblest Pomp her earliest Stage.

Preserv'd thro' Time, the speaking Scenes impart

Each changeful Wish of *Phædra*'s tortur'd Heart :

Or paint the Curse, that mark'd the * *Theban*'s Reign,

A Bed incestuous, and a Father slain.

Line after Line, our pitying Eyes o'erflow,

Trace the sad Tale, and own another's Woe.

* The *Œdipus* of *Sophocles*.

To *Rome* remov'd, with equal Pow'r to please,
The *Comic* Sisters kept their native Ease.   40
With jealous Fear declining *Greece* beheld
Her own *Menander*'s Art almost excell'd !
But ev'ry Muse essay'd to raise in vain
Some labour'd Rival of her *Tragic* Strain ;
Ilissus' Laurels, tho' transferr'd with Toil,
Droop'd their fair Leaves, nor knew th' unfriendly Soil.

When *Rome* herself, her envy'd Glories dead,
No more Imperial, stoop'd her conquer'd Head :
Luxuriant *Florence* chose a softer Theme,
While all was Peace, by *Arno*'s silver Stream.   50
With sweeter Notes th' *Etrurian* Vales complain'd,
And Arts reviving told—a *Cosmo* reign'd.
Their wanton Lyres the Bards of *Provence* strung,
Sweet flow'd the Lays, but Love was all they sung.
The gay Description could not fail to move,
For, led by Nature, all are Friends to Love.

But Heav'n, still rising in its Works, decreed
The perfect Boast of Time should last succeed.
The beauteous Union must appear at length,
Of *Tuscan* Fancy, and *Athenian* Strength :   60
One greater Muse *Eliza*'s Reign adorn,
And ev'n a *Shakespear* to her Fame be born !

Yet ah ! so bright her Morning's op'ning Ray,
In vain our *Britain* hop'd an equal Day !
No second Growth the Western Isle could bear,
At once exhausted with too rich a Year.
Too nicely *Johnson* knew the Critic's Part ;
Nature in him was almost lost in Art.
Of softer Mold the gentle *Fletcher* came,
The next in Order, as the next in Name.   70
With pleas'd Attention 'midst his Scenes we find
Each glowing Thought, that warms the Female Mind ;
Each melting Sigh, and ev'ry tender Tear,
The Lover's Wishes and the Virgin's Fear.
His * ev'ry Strain the Loves and Graces own ;
But stronger *Shakespear* felt for *Man* alone :
Drawn by his Pen, our ruder Passions stand
Th' unrivall'd Picture of his early Hand.

With gradual Steps, and slow, exacter *France*
Saw Art's fair Empire o'er her Shores advance :   80
By length of Toil, a bright Perfection knew,
Correctly bold, and just in all she drew.
Till late *Corneille* from Epick † *Lucan* brought
The full Expression, and the *Roman* Thought ;

* Their Characters are thus distinguish'd by Mr. *Dryden.*
† The favourite Author of the Elder *Corneille.*

And classic Judgment gain'd to sweet *Racine*
The temp'rate Strength of *Maro*'s chaster Line.

But wilder far the *British* Laurel spread,
And Wreaths less artful crown our Poet's Head.
Yet He alone to ev'ry Scene could give
Th' Historian's Truth, and bid the Manners live.   90
Wak'd at his Call I view, with glad Surprize,
Majestic Forms of mighty Monarchs rise.
There *Henry*'s Trumpets spread their loud Alarms,
And laurel'd Conquest waits her Hero's Arms.
Here gentler *Edward* claims a pitying Sigh,
Scarce born to Honours, and so soon to die !
Yet shall thy Throne, unhappy Infant, bring
No Beam of Comfort to the guilty King ?
The * Time shall come, when *Glo'ster*'s Heart shall bleed
In Life's last Hours, with Horror of the Deed :   100
When dreary Visions shall at last present
Thy vengeful Image, in the midnight Tent :
Thy Hand unseen the secret Death shall bear,
Blunt the weak Sword, and break th' oppressive Spear.

Where'er we turn, by Fancy charm'd, we find
Some sweet Illusion of the cheated Mind.

* Tempus erit Turno, magno cum optaverit emptum
  Intactum Pallanta, &c.

Oft, wild of Wing, she calls the Soul to rove
With humbler Nature, in the rural Grove ;
Where Swains contented own the quiet Scene,
And twilight Fairies tread the circled Green :   110
Drest by her Hand, the Woods and Vallies smile,
And Spring diffusive decks th' *enchanted Isle.*

  O blest in all that Genius gives to charm,
Whose Morals mend us, and whose Passions warm !
Oft let my Youth attend thy various Page,
Where rich Invention rules th' unbounded Stage.
There ev'ry Scene the Poet's Warmth may raise,
And melting Music find the softest Lays.
O might the Muse with equal Ease persuade
Expressive Picture to adopt thine Aid !   120
Some pow'rful *Raphael* shou'd again appear,
And Arts consenting fix their Empire here.

  Methinks ev'n now I view some fair Design,
Where breathing Nature lives in ev'ry Line :
Chaste, and subdu'd, the modest Colours lie,
In fair Proportion to th' approving Eye.—
And see, where * *Antony* lamenting stands
In fixt Distress, and spreads his pleading Hands !

      * See the Tragedy of *Julius Caesar.*

O'er the pale Corse the Warrior seems to bend,
Deep sunk in Grief, and mourns his murther'd Friend !
Still as they press, he calls on all around,   131
Lifts the torn Robe, and points the bleeding Wound.

But * who is he, whose Brows exalted bear
A Rage impatient, and a fiercer Air ?
Ev'n now, his Thoughts with eager Vengeance doom
The last sad Ruin of ungrateful *Rome*.
Till, slow-advancing o'er the tented Plain,
In sable Weeds, appear the Kindred-train :
The frantic Mother leads their wild Despair,
Beats her swoln Breast, and rends her silver Hair.   140
And see he yields ! . . . the Tears unbidden start,
And conscious Nature claims th' unwilling Heart !
O'er all the Man conflicting Passions rise,
Rage grasps the Sword, while *Pity* melts the Eyes.

Thus, gen'rous Critic, as thy Bard inspires,
The Sister Arts shall nurse their drooping Fires ;
Each from his Scenes her Stores alternate bring,
Spread the fair Tints, or wake the vocal String :
Those *Sibyl*-Leaves, the Sport of ev'ry Wind,
(For Poets ever were a careless Kind)   150

* *Coriolanus.*   See Mr. *Spence*'s Dialogues on the *Odyssey.*

By thee dispos'd, no farther Toil demand,
But, just to Nature, own thy forming Hand.

So spread o'er *Greece*, th' harmonious Whole unknown,
Ev'n *Homer's* Numbers charm'd by Parts alone.
Their own *Ulysses* scarce had wander'd more,
By Winds and Waters cast on ev'ry Shore :
When, rais'd by Fate, some former *Hanmer* join'd
Each beauteous Image of the tuneful Mind :
And bad, like Thee, his *Athens* ever claim
A fond Alliance with the Poet's Name.   160

Oxford, Dec. 3,
1743.

FINIS.

O D E S

ON SEVERAL

Defcriptive and *Allegoric*

S U B J E C T S.

By WILLIAM COLLINS.

——Ειην
Ευρησιεπης αναγεισθαι
Προσφορος εν Μοισᾶν Διφρω·
Τολμα δε και αμφιλαφης Δυναμις
Εσποιτο.——

Πινδαρ, Ολυμπ. Θ.

L O N D O N:
Printed for A. MILLAR, in the *Strand*.
M.DCC.XLVII.
(Price One Shilling.)

O D E *to* P I T Y.

O THOU, the Friend of Man assign'd,
With balmy Hands his Wounds to bind,
    And charm his frantic Woe:
When first *Distress* with Dagger keen
Broke forth to waste his destin'd Scene,
    His wild unsated Foe!

2.

By *Pella's* * Bard, a magic Name,
By all the Griefs his Thought could frame,
    Receive my humble Rite:
Long, *Pity*, let the Nations view   10
Thy sky-worn Robes of tend'rest Blue,
    And Eyes of dewy Light!

3.

But wherefore need I wander wide
To old *Ilissus*' distant Side,

  * *Euripides*, of whom *Aristotle* pronounces, on a Comparison of
him with *Sophocles*, That he was the greater Master of the tender
Passions, ἦν τραγικώτερος.

Deserted Stream, and mute ?
Wild *Arun* * too has heard thy Strains,
And Echo, 'midst my native Plains,
    Been sooth'd by *Pity*'s Lute.

4.

There first the Wren thy Myrtles shed
On gentlest *Otway*'s infant Head,   20
    To Him thy Cell was shown ;
And while He sung the Female Heart,
With Youth's soft Notes unspoil'd by Art,
    Thy Turtles mix'd their own.

5.

Come, *Pity*, come, by Fancy's Aid,
Ev'n now my Thoughts, relenting Maid,
    Thy Temple's Pride design :
Its Southern Site, its Truth compleat
Shall raise a wild Enthusiast Heat,
    In all who view the Shrine.   30

6.

There Picture's Toils shall well relate,
How Chance, or hard involving Fate,

  * The River *Arun* runs by the Village in *Sussex*, where *Otway*
had his Birth.

O'er mortal Bliss prevail :
The Buskin'd Muse shall near her stand,
And sighing prompt her tender Hand.
    With each disastrous Tale.

7.

There let me oft, retir'd by Day,
In Dreams of Passion melt away,
    Allow'd with Thee to dwell :
There waste the mournful Lamp of Night,   40
Till, Virgin, Thou again delight
    To hear a *British* Shell !

ODE *to* FEAR.

[STROPHE]

THOU, to whom the World unknown
With all its shadowy Shapes is shown ;
Who see'st appall'd th' unreal Scene,
While Fancy lifts the Veil between :

    Ah *Fear !* Ah frantic *Fear !*

    I see, I see Thee near.

I know thy hurried Step, thy haggard Eye !
Like Thee I start, like Thee disorder'd fly,
For lo what *Monsters* in thy Train appear !
Danger, whose Limbs of Giant Mold   **10**
What mortal Eye can fix'd behold ?
Who stalks his Round, an hideous Form,
Howling amidst the Midnight Storm,
Or throws him on the ridgy Steep
Of some loose hanging Rock to sleep :
And with him thousand Phantoms join'd,
Who prompt to Deeds accurs'd the Mind :
And those, the Fiends, who near allied,
O'er Nature's Wounds, and Wrecks preside ;
Whilst *Vengeance*, in the lurid Air,   &c

Lifts her red Arm, expos'd and bare :
On whom that rav'ning * Brood of Fate,
Who lap the Blood of Sorrow, wait ;
Who, *Fear*, this ghastly Train can see,
And look not madly wild, like Thee ?

E P O D E.

In earliest *Grece* to Thee with partial Choice,
  The Grief-full Muse addrest her infant Tongue ;
The Maids and Matrons, on her awful Voice,
  Silent and pale in wild Amazement hung.

Yet He, the Bard † who first invok'd thy Name,   30
  Disdain'd in *Marathon* its Pow'r to feel :
For not alone he nurs'd the Poet's flame,
  But reach'd from Virtue's Hand the Patriot's Steel.

But who is He whom later Garlands grace,
  Who left a-while o'er *Hybla*'s Dews to rove,
With trembling Eyes thy dreary Steps to trace,
  Where Thou and *Furies* shar'd the baleful Grove ?

* Alluding to the Κύνας ἀφύκτους of *Sophocles*. See the ELECTRA.
† *Æschylus.*

Wrapt in thy cloudy Veil th' *Incestuous Queen* *

 Sigh'd the sad Call † her Son and Husband hear'd,

When once alone it broke the silent Scene,   40

 And He the Wretch of *Thebes* no more appear'd.

O *Fear*, I know Thee by my throbbing Heart,

 Thy with'ring Pow'r inspir'd each mournful Line,

Tho' gentle *Pity* claim her mingled Part,

 Yet all the Thunders of the Scene are thine !

ANTISTROPHE.

Thou who such weary Lengths hast past,

Where wilt thou rest, mad Nymph, at last ?

Say, wilt thou shroud in haunted Cell,

Where gloomy *Rape* and *Murder* dwell ?

 Or in some hollow'd Seat,   50

 'Gainst which the big Waves beat,

Hear drowning Sea-men's Cries in Tempests brought !

Dark Pow'r, with shudd'ring meek submitted Thought

---

 * *Jocasta.*

     † οὐδ' ἔτ' ὠρώρει βοή,

   Ἦν μέν σιωπή, φθέγμα δ' ἐξαίφνης τινὸς

   Θωΰξεν αὐτόν, ὥστε πάντας ὀρθίας

   Στῆσαι φόβῳ δείσαντας ἐξαίφνης τρίχας.

      See the Œdip. Colon. of *Sophocles.*

Be mine, to read the Visions old,
Which thy awak'ning Bards have told:
And lest thou meet my blasted View,
Hold each strange Tale devoutly true;
Ne'er be I found, by Thee o'eraw'd,
In that thrice-hallow'd Eve abroad,
When Ghosts, as Cottage-Maids believe,   60
Their pebbled Beds permitted leave,
And *Gobblins* haunt from Fire, or Fen,
Or Mine, or Flood, the Walks of Men!

  O Thou whose Spirit most possest
The sacred Seat of *Shakespear*'s Breast!
By all that from thy Prophet broke,
In thy Divine Emotions spoke:
Hither again thy Fury deal,
Teach me but once like Him to feel:
His *Cypress Wreath* my Meed decree,   70
And I, O *Fear*, will dwell with *Thee!*

O D E *to* SIMPLICITY.

1.

O THOU by *Nature* taught,
  To breathe her genuine Thought,
In Numbers warmly pure, and sweetly strong:
  Who first on Mountains wild,
  In *Fancy* loveliest Child,
Thy Babe, or *Pleasure*'s, nurs'd the Pow'rs of Song!

2.

  Thou, who with Hermit Heart
  Disdain'st the Wealth of Art,
And Gauds, and pageant Weeds, and trailing Pall:
  But com'st a decent Maid   10
  In *Attic* Robe array'd,
O chaste unboastful Nymph, to Thee I call!

3.

By all the honey'd Store

On *Hybla*'s Thymy Shore,

By all her Blooms, and mingled Murmurs dear,

   By Her *, whose Love-lorn Woe

   In Ev'ning Musings slow

Sooth'd sweetly sad *Electra*'s Poet's Ear :

4.

By old *Cephisus* deep,

   Who spread his wavy Sweep   20

In warbled Wand'rings round thy green Retreat,

   On whose enamel'd Side

   When holy *Freedom* died

No equal Haunt allur'd thy future Feet.

5.

O Sister meek of Truth,

   To my admiring Youth,

Thy sober Aid and native Charms infuse !

   The Flow'rs that sweetest breathe,

   Tho' Beauty cull'd the Wreath,

Still ask thy Hand to range their order'd Hues.   30

* The ἀηδών, or Nightingale, for which *Sophocles* seems to have entertain'd a peculiar Fondness.

6.

While *Rome* could none esteem
  But Virtue's Patriot Theme,
You lov'd her Hills, and led her Laureate Band :
  But staid to sing alone
  To one distinguish'd Throne,
And turn'd thy Face, and fled her alter'd Land.

7.

No more, in Hall or Bow'r,
  The Passions own thy Pow'r,
Love, only Love her forceless Numbers mean :
  For Thou hast left her Shrine,   40
  Nor Olive more, nor Vine,
Shall gain thy Feet to bless the servile Scene.

8.

Tho' Taste, tho' Genius bless,
  To some divine Excess,
Faints the cold Work till Thou inspire the whole ;
  What each, what all supply,
  May court, may charm our Eye,
Thou, only Thou can'st raise the meeting Soul !

9.

   Of These let others ask,
   To aid some mighty Task,   50
I only seek to find thy temp'rate Vale :
   Where oft my Reed might sound
   To Maids and Shepherds round,
And all thy Sons, O *Nature*, learn my Tale

ODE *on the* POETICAL CHARACTER.

[STROPHE]

As once, if not with light Regard
I read aright that gifted Bard,
(Him whose School above the rest
His Loveliest *Elfin* Queen has blest.)
One, only One, unrival'd Fair *,
Might hope the magic Girdle wear,
At solemn Turney hung on high,
The Wish of each love-darting Eye;

Lo! to each other Nymph in turn applied,
   As if, in Air unseen, some hov'ring Hand,   10
Some chaste and Angel-Friend to Virgin-Fame,
   With whisper'd Spell had burst the starting Band,
It left unblest her loath'd dishonour'd Side;
     Happier hopeless Fair, if never
     Her baffled Hand with vain Endeavour
Had touch'd that fatal Zone to her denied!

* *Florimel*. See *Spenser* Leg. 4th.

Young *Fancy* thus, to me Divinest Name,

    To whom, prepar'd and bath'd in Heav'n,

    The Cest of amplest Pow'r is giv'n :

    To few the God-like Gift assigns,   20

    To gird their blest prophetic Loins,

And gaze her Visions wild, and feel unmix'd her Flame !

[EPODE]

2.

The Band, as Fairy Legends say,

Was wove on that creating Day,

When He, who call'd with Thought to Birth

Yon tented Sky, this laughing Earth,

And drest with Springs, and Forests tall,

And pour'd the Main engirting all,

Long by the lov'd *Enthusiast* woo'd,

Himself in some Diviner Mood,   30

Retiring, sate with her alone,

And plac'd her on his Saphire Throne,

The whiles, the vaulted Shrine around,

Seraphic Wires were heard to sound,

Now sublimest Triumph swelling,

Now on Love and Mercy dwelling ;

And she, from out the veiling Cloud,

Breath'd her magic Notes aloud :

And Thou, Thou rich-hair'd Youth of Morn,
And all thy subject Life was born !   40
The dang'rous Passions kept aloof,
Far from the sainted growing Woof :
But near it sate Ecstatic *Wonder*,
List'ning the deep applauding Thunder :
And *Truth*, in sunny Vest array'd,
By whose the Tarsel's Eyes were made ;
All the shad'wy Tribes of *Mind*,
In braided Dance their Murmurs join'd,
And all the bright uncounted *Pow'rs*,
Who feed on Heav'n's ambrosial Flow'rs.   50
Where is the Bard, whose Soul can now
Its high presuming Hopes avow ?
Where He who thinks, with Rapture blind,
This hallow'd Work for Him design'd ?

[ANTISTROPHE]

3.

High on some Cliff, to Heav'n up-pil'd,
Of rude Access, of Prospect wild,
Where, tangled round the jealous Steep,
Strange Shades o'erbrow the Valleys deep,
And holy *Genii* guard the Rock,
Its Gloomes embrown, its Springs unlock,   60

While on its rich ambitious Head,
An *Eden*, like his own, lies spread :

I view that Oak, the fancied Glades among,
 By which as *Milton* lay, His Ev'ning Ear,
From many a Cloud that drop'd Ethereal Dew,
 Nigh spher'd in Heav'n its native Strains could hear :
On which that ancient Trump he reach'd was hung ;
  Thither oft his Glory greeting,
  From *Waller*'s Myrtle Shades retreating,
With many a Vow from Hope's aspiring Tongue,   70

My trembling Feet his guiding Steps pursue ;
  In vain—Such Bliss to One alone,
  Of all the Sons of Soul was known,
  And Heav'n, and *Fancy*, kindred Pow'rs,
  Have now o'erturn'd th' inspiring Bow'rs,
Or curtain'd close such Scene from ev'ry future View.

O D E,

Written in the beginning of the Year 1746.

How sleep the Brave, who sink to Rest,
By all their Country's Wishes blest !
When *Spring*, with dewy Fingers cold,
Returns to deck their hallow'd Mold,
She there shall dress a sweeter Sod,
Than *Fancy*'s Feet have ever trod.

2.

By Fairy Hands their Knell is rung,
By Forms unseen their Dirge is sung ;
There *Honour* comes, a Pilgrim grey,
To bless the Turf that wraps their Clay,   10
And *Freedom* shall a-while repair,
To dwell a weeping Hermit there !

O D E *to* MERCY.

[Written in 1746.]

STROPHE.

O Thou, who sit'st a smiling Bride
By *Valour*'s arm'd and awful Side,
Gentlest of Sky-born Forms, and best ador'd :
  Who oft with Songs, divine to hear,
  Win'st from his fatal Grasp the Spear,
And hid'st in Wreaths of Flow'rs his bloodless Sword !

Thou who, amidst the deathful Field,
  By Godlike Chiefs alone beheld,
Oft with thy Bosom bare art found,
Pleading for him the Youth who sinks to Ground :   10
  See, *Mercy*, see, with pure and loaded Hands,
  Before thy Shrine my Country's Genius stands,
And decks thy Altar still, tho' pierc'd with many a Wound!

ANTISTROPHE.

When he whom ev'n our Joys provoke,
The *Fiend of Nature* join'd his Yoke,
And rush'd in Wrath to make our Isle his Prey;
Thy Form, from out thy sweet Abode,
O'ertook Him on his blasted Road,
And stop'd his Wheels, and look'd his Rage away.

I see recoil his sable Steeds,   20
That bore Him swift to Salvage Deeds,
Thy tender melting Eyes they own;
O Maid, for all thy Love to *Britain* shown,
Where *Justice* bars her Iron Tow'r,
To Thee we build a roseate Bow'r,
Thou, Thou shalt rule our Queen, and share our Mon-
arch's Throne!

ODE *to* LIBERTY.

STROPHE.

WHO shall awake the *Spartan* Fife,

And call in solemn Sounds to Life,

The Youths, whose Locks divinely spreading,

  Like vernal Hyacinths in sullen Hue,

At once the Breath of Fear and Virtue shedding,

  Applauding *Freedom* lov'd of old to view ?

What New *Alcæus* *, Fancy-blest,

Shall sing the Sword, in Myrtles drest,

  At *Wisdom*'s Shrine a-while its Flame concealing,

(What Place so fit to seal a Deed renown'd ?)   10

  Till she her brightest Lightnings round revealing,

It leap'd in Glory forth, and dealt her prompted Wound !

---

* Alluding to that beautiful Fragment of *Alcæus*.

      Ἐν μύρτου κλαδὶ τὸ ξίφος φορήσω,

      Ὥσπερ Ἁρμόδιος καὶ Ἀριστογείτων.

      Φίλταθ' Ἁρμόδι, οὔπω τέθνηκας,

      Νήσοις δ' ἐν Μακάρων σέ φασιν εἶναι.

      Ἐν μύρτου κλαδὶ τὸ ξίφος φορήσω,

      Ὥσπερ Ἁρμόδιος καὶ Ἀριστογείτων,

      Ὅτ' Ἀθηναίης ἐν θυσίαις

      Ἄνδρα τύραννον Ἵππαρχον ἐκαινέτην.

      Ἀεὶ σφῶν κλέος ἔσσεται κατ' αἶαν,

      Φίλταθ' Ἁρμόδι, καὶ Ἀριστογείτων.

O Goddess, in that feeling Hour,

   When most its Sounds would court thy Ears,

     Let not my Shell's misguided Pow'r *

   E'er draw thy sad, thy mindful Tears.

No, *Freedom*, no, I will not tell,

  How *Rome*, before thy weeping Face,

With heaviest Sound, a Giant-statue, fell,

  Push'd by a wild and artless Race,   20

  From off its wide ambitious Base,

When Time his Northern Sons of Spoil awoke,

   And all the blended Work of Strength and Grace,

    With many a rude repeated Stroke,

And many a barb'rous Yell, to thousand Fragments broke.

E P O D E.

2.

Yet ev'n, where'er the least appear'd,

Th' admiring World thy Hand rever'd ;

Still 'midst the scatter'd States around,

Some Remnants of Her Strength were found ;

They saw by what escap'd the Storm,   30

How wond'rous rose her perfect Form ;

---

* Μὴ μὴ ταῦτα λέγωμες, ἃ δάκρυον ἤγαγε Δηοῖ.

                        Callimach. Ὕμνος εἰς Δήμητρα.

How in the great the labour'd Whole,

Each mighty Master pour'd his Soul!

For sunny *Florence*, Seat of Art,

Beneath her Vines preserv'd a part,

Till They *, whom Science lov'd to name,

(O who could fear it?) quench'd her Flame.

And lo, an humbler Relick laid

In jealous *Pisa*'s Olive Shade!

See small *Marino* † joins the Theme,   40

Tho' least, not last in thy Esteem:

Strike, louder strike th' ennobling Strings

To those ‡, whose Merchant Sons were Kings;

To Him §, who deck'd with pearly Pride,

In *Adria* weds his green-hair'd Bride;

Hail Port of Glory, Wealth, and Pleasure,

Ne'er let me change this *Lydian* Measure:

Nor e'er her former Pride relate,

To sad *Liguria*'s ‖ bleeding State.

Ah no! more pleas'd thy Haunts I seek,   50

On wild *Helvetia*'s ¶ Mountains bleak:

(Where, when the favor'd of thy Choice,

The daring Archer heard thy Voice;

* The Family of the *Medici*.
† The little Republic of *San Marino*.
‡ The *Venetians*.   § The Doge of *Venice*.
‖ *Genoa*.   ¶ *Switzerland*.

Forth from his Eyrie rous'd in Dread,

The rav'ning *Eagle* northward fled.)

Or dwell in willow'd Meads more near,

With Those * to whom Thy Stork is dear:

Those whom the Rod of *Alva* bruis'd,

Whose Crown a *British* Queen † refus'd!

The Magic works, Thou feel'st the Strains,   60

One holier Name alone remains;

The perfect Spell shall then avail,

Hail Nymph, ador'd by *Britain*, Hail!

ANTISTROPHE.

Beyond the Measure vast of Thought,

The Works, the Wizzard *Time* has wrought!

The *Gaul*, 'tis held of antique Story,

Saw *Britain* link'd to his now adverse Strand ‡,

No Sea between, nor Cliff sublime and hoary,

* The *Dutch*, amongst whom there are very severe Penalties for those who are convicted of killing this Bird. They are kept tame in almost all their Towns, and particularly at the *Hague*, of the Arms of which they make a Part. The common People of *Holland* are said to entertain a superstitious Sentiment, That if the whole Species of them should become extinct, they should lose their Liberties.   † Queen *Elizabeth*.

‡ This Tradition is mention'd by several of our old Historians. Some Naturalists too have endeavour'd to support the Probability of the Fact, by Arguments drawn from the correspondent Disposition of the two opposite Coasts. I don't remember that any Poetical Use has been hitherto made of it.

He pass'd with unwet Feet thro' all our Land.

   To the blown *Baltic* then, they say,   70

   The wild Waves found another way,

Where *Orcas* howls, his wolfish Mountains rounding ;

   Till all the banded West at once 'gan rise,

A wide wild Storm ev'n Nature's self confounding,

   With'ring her Giant Sons with strange uncouth Sur-
      prise.

   This pillar'd Earth so firm and wide,

     By Winds and inward Labors torn,

   In Thunders dread was push'd aside,

     And down the should'ring Billows born.

And see, like Gems, her laughing Train,   80

   The little Isles on ev'ry side,

Mona *, once hid from those who search the Main,

   Where thousand Elfin Shapes abide,

   And *Wight* who checks the west'ring Tide,

---

* There is a Tradition in the Isle of *Man*, that a Mermaid becoming enamour'd of a young Man of extraordinary Beauty, took an Opportunity of meeting him one day as he walked on the Shore, and open'd her Passion to him, but was receiv'd with a Coldness, occasion'd by his Horror and Surprize at her Appearance. This however was so misconstrued by the Sea-Lady, that in revenge for his Treatment of her, she punish'd the whole Island, by covering it with a Mist, so that all who attempted to carry on any Commerce with it, either never arriv'd at it, but wander'd up and down the Sea, or were on a sudden wreck'd upon its Cliffs.

For Thee consenting Heav'n has each bestow'd,
A fair Attendant on her sov'reign Pride:
To Thee this blest Divorce she ow'd,
For thou hast made her Vales thy lov'd, thy last Abode!

SECOND EPODE.

Then too, 'tis said, an hoary Pile,
'Midst the green Navel of our Isle,   90
Thy Shrine in some religious Wood,
O Soul-enforcing Goddess stood!
There oft the painted Native's Feet,
Were wont thy Form celestial meet:
Tho' now with hopeless Toil we trace
Time's backward Rolls, to find its place;
Whether the fiery-tressed *Dane*,
Or *Roman*'s self o'erturn'd the Fane,
Or in what Heav'n-left Age it fell,
'Twere hard for modern Song to tell.   100
Yet still, if Truth those Beams infuse,
Which guide at once, and charm the Muse,
Beyond yon braided Clouds that lie,
Paving the light-embroider'd Sky:
Amidst the bright pavilion'd Plains,

The beauteous *Model* still remains.

There happier than in Islands blest,

Or Bow'rs by Spring or *Hebe* drest,

The Chiefs who fill our *Albion*'s Story,

In warlike Weeds, retir'd in Glory,   110

Hear their consorted *Druids* sing

Their Triumphs to th' immortal String.

  How may the Poet now unfold

What never Tongue or Numbers told ?

How learn delighted, and amaz'd,

What Hands unknown that Fabric rais'd ?

Ev'n now before his favor'd Eyes,

In *Gothic* Pride it seems to rise !

Yet *Græcia*'s graceful Orders join,

Majestic thro' the mix'd Design ;   120

The secret Builder knew to chuse,

Each sphere-found Gem of richest Hues :

Whate'er Heav'n's purer Mold contains,

When nearer Suns emblaze its Veins ;

There on the Walls the *Patriot*'s Sight,

May ever hang with fresh Delight,

And, grav'd with some Prophetic Rage,

Read *Albion*'s Fame thro' ev'ry Age.

  Ye Forms Divine, ye Laureate Band,

That near her inmost Altar stand !   130

Now sooth Her, to her blissful Train
Blithe *Concord*'s social Form to gain :
Concord, whose Myrtle Wand can steep
Ev'n *Anger*'s blood-shot Eyes in Sleep :
Before whose breathing Bosom's Balm,
Rage drops his Steel, and Storms grow calm ;
Her let our Sires and Matrons hoar
Welcome to *Britain*'s ravag'd Shore,
Our Youths, enamour'd of the Fair,
Play with the Tangles of her Hair,   140
Till in one loud applauding Sound,
The Nations shout to Her around,
O how supremely art thou blest,
Thou, Lady, Thou shalt rule the West !

O D E, *to a Lady on the Death of Colonel* R o s s *in the Action of* Fontenoy.

[Written in May 1745 and addressed to Miss Elizabeth Goddard of Harting in Sussex. First published in Dodsley's *Museum,* June 7, 1746.]

I.

WHILE, lost to all his former Mirth,
Britannia's Genius bends to Earth,
  And mourns the fatal Day :
While stain'd with Blood he strives to tear
Unseemly from his Sea-green Hair
  The Wreaths of chearful *May :*

2.

The Thoughts which musing Pity pays,
And fond Remembrance loves to raise,
  Your faithful Hours attend :
Still Fancy to Herself unkind,   10
Awakes to Grief the soften'd Mind,
  And points the bleeding Friend.

3.

By rapid *Scheld*'s descending Wave
His Country's Vows shall bless the Grave,
  Where'er the Youth is laid :
That sacred Spot the Village Hind
With ev'ry sweetest Turf shall bind,
  And Peace protect the Shade.

4.

Blest Youth, regardful of thy Doom,
Aërial Hands shall build thy Tomb,   20
  With shadowy Trophies crown'd :
Whilst *Honor* bath'd in Tears shall rove
To sigh thy Name thro' ev'ry Grove,
  And call his Heros round.

5.

The warlike Dead of ev'ry Age,
Who fill the fair recording Page,
  Shall leave their sainted Rest :
And, half-reclining on his Spear,
Each wond'ring Chief by turns appear,
  To hail the blooming Guest.   30

6.

Old *Edward*'s Sons, unknown to yield,
Shall croud from *Cressy*'s laurell'd Field,
    And gaze with fix'd Delight:
Again for *Britain*'s Wrongs they feel,
Again they snatch the gleamy Steel,
    And wish th' avenging Fight.

7.

But lo where, sunk in deep Despair,
Her Garments torn, her Bosom bare.
    Impatient *Freedom* lies !
Her matted Tresses madly spread,
To ev'ry Sod, which wraps the Dead,
    She turns her joyless Eyes.

8.

Ne'er shall she leave that lowly Ground,
Till Notes of Triumph bursting round
    Proclaim her Reign restor'd:
Till *William* seek the sad Retreat,
And bleeding at her sacred Feet,
    Present the sated Sword.

9.

If, weak to sooth so soft an Heart,

These pictur'd Glories nought impart,　　　　50

　　　To dry thy constant Tear :

If yet, in Sorrow's distant Eye,

Expos'd and pale thou see'st him lie,

　　　Wild War insulting near :

10.

Where'er from Time Thou court'st Relief,

The Muse shall still, with social Grief,

　　　Her gentlest Promise keep :

Ev'n humble *Harting*'s cottag'd Vale

Shall learn the sad repeated Tale,

　　　And bid her Shepherds weep.　　　　60

ODE *to* EVENING.

IF ought of Oaten Stop, or Pastoral Song,
May hope, O pensive *Eve*, to sooth thine Ear,
    Like thy own brawling Springs,
    Thy Springs, and dying Gales,
O *Nymph* reserv'd, while now the bright-hair'd Sun
Sits in yon western Tent, whose cloudy Skirts,
    With Brede ethereal wove,
    O'erhang his wavy Bed :
Now Air is hush'd, save where the weak-ey'd Bat,
With short shrill Shriek flits by on leathern Wing,   10
    Or where the Beetle winds
    His small but sullen Horn,
As oft he rises 'midst the twilight Path,
Against the Pilgrim born in heedless Hum :
    Now teach me, *Maid* compos'd,
    To breathe some soften'd Strain,
Whose Numbers stealing thro' thy darkning Vale,
May not unseemly with its Stillness suit,
    As musing slow, I hail
    Thy genial lov'd Return !   20

For when thy folding Star arising shews
His paly Circlet, at his warning Lamp
    The fragrant *Hours*, and *Elves*
    Who slept in Buds the Day,
And many a *Nymph* who wreaths her Brows with Sedge,
And sheds the fresh'ning Dew, and lovelier still,
    The *Pensive Pleasures* sweet
    Prepare thy shadowy Car.
Then let me rove some wild and heathy Scene,
Or find some Ruin 'midst its dreary Dells,   30
    Whose Walls more awful nod
    By thy religious Gleams.
Or if chill blustring Winds, or driving Rain,
Prevent my willing Feet, be mine the Hut,
    That from the Mountain's Side,
    Views Wilds, and swelling Floods,
And Hamlets brown, and dim-discover'd Spires,
And hears their simple Bell, and marks o'er all
    Thy Dewy Fingers draw
    The gradual dusky Veil.   40

While *Spring* shall pour his Show'rs, as oft he wont,
And bathe thy breathing Tresses, meekest *Eve !*
    While *Summer* loves to sport,
    Beneath thy ling'ring Light:

While sallow *Autumn* fills thy Lap with Leaves,

Or *Winter* yelling thro' the troublous Air,

    Affrights thy shrinking Train,

    And rudely rends thy Robes.

So long regardful of thy quiet Rule,

Shall *Fancy*, *Friendship*, *Science*, smiling *Peace*,   50

    Thy gentlest Influence own,

    And love thy fav'rite Name !

O D E *to* P E A C E.

O THOU, who bad'st thy Turtles bear
Swift from his Grasp thy golden Hair,
 And sought'st thy native Skies :
When *War*, by Vultures drawn from far,
To *Britain* bent his Iron Car,
 And bad his Storms arise !

2.

Tir'd of his rude tyrannic Sway,
Our Youth shall fix some festive Day,
 His sullen Shrines to burn :
But Thou who hear'st the turning Spheres, 10
What Sounds may charm thy partial Ears,
 And gain thy blest Return !

3.

O *Peace*, thy injur'd Robes up-bind,
O rise, and leave not one behind
 Of all thy beamy Train :

The *British* Lion, Goddess sweet,
Lies stretch'd on Earth to kiss thy Feet,
   And own thy holier Reign.

4.

Let others court thy transient Smile,
But come to grace thy western Isle,   20
   By warlike *Honour* led !
And, while around her Ports rejoice,
While all her Sons adore thy Choice,
   With Him for ever wed !

The MANNERS. *An* ODE.

FAREWELL, for clearer Ken design'd,
The dim-discover'd Tracts of Mind :
Truths which, from Action's Paths retir'd,
My silent Search in vain requir'd !
No more my Sail that Deep explores,
No more I search those magic Shores,
What Regions part the World of Soul,
Or whence thy Streams, *Opinion*, roll :
If e'er I round such Fairy Field,
Some Pow'r impart the Spear and Shield,   10
At which the Wizzard *Passions* fly,
By which the Giant *Follies* die !

    Farewell the Porch, whose Roof is seen,
Arch'd with th' enlivening Olive's Green :
Where *Science*, prank'd in tissued Vest,
By *Reason*, *Pride*, and *Fancy* drest,
Comes like a Bride so trim array'd,
To wed with *Doubt* in *Plato*'s Shade !

Youth of the quick uncheated Sight,
Thy Walks, *Observance*, more invite !   20
O Thou, who lov'st that ampler Range,
Where Life's wide Prospects round thee change,
And with her mingling Sons ally'd,
Throw'st the prattling Page aside :
To me in Converse sweet impart,
To read in Man the native Heart,
To learn, where Science sure is found,
From Nature as she lives around :
And gazing oft her Mirror true,
By turns each shifting Image view !   30
Till meddling *Art*'s officious Lore,
Reverse the Lessons taught before,
Alluring from a safer Rule,
To dream in her enchanted School ;
Tho' Heav'n, whate'er of Great we boast,
Has blest this social Science most.

Retiring hence to thoughtful Cell,
As *Fancy* breathes her potent Spell,
Not vain she finds the charmful Task,
In Pageant quaint, in motley Mask,   40
Behold before her musing Eyes,
The countless *Manners* round her rise ;
While ever varying as they pass,

To some *Contempt* applies her Glass :
With these the *white-rob'd Maids* combine,
And those the laughing *Satyrs* join !
But who is He whom now she views,
In Robe of wild contending Hues ?
Tho' by the Passions nurs'd, I greet
The comic Sock that binds thy Feet ! 50
O *Humour*, Thou whose Name is known
To *Britain*'s favor'd Isle alone :
Me too amidst thy Band admit,
There where the young-eyed healthful *Wit*,
(Whose Jewels in his crisped Hair
Are plac'd each other's Beams to share,
Whom no Delights from Thee divide)
In Laughter loos'd attends thy Side !

By old *Miletus* * who so long
Has ceas'd his Love-inwoven Song : 60
By all you taught the *Tuscan* Maids,
In chang'd *Italia*'s modern Shades :
By Him †, whose *Knight*'s distinguish'd Name
Refin'd a Nation's Lust of Fame ;
Whose Tales ev'n now, with Echos sweet,
Castilia's *Moorish* Hills repeat :

* Alluding to the *Milesian* Tales, some of the earliest Romances.
† *Cervantes.*

Or Him *, whom *Seine*'s blue Nymphs deplore,

In watchet Weeds on *Gallia*'s Shore,

Who drew the sad *Sicilian* Maid,

By Virtues in her Sire betray'd :   70

  O Nature boon, from whom proceed

Each forceful Thought, each prompted Deed ;

If but from Thee I hope to feel,

On all my Heart imprint thy Seal !

Let some retreating Cynic find,

Those oft-turn'd Scrolls I leave behind,

The *Sports* and I this Hour agree,

To rove thy Scene-full World with Thee !

  * Monsieur *Le Sage*, Author of the incomparable Adventures of *Gil Blas de Santillane*, who died in *Paris* in the Year 1745 [actually 1747].

The PASSIONS. *An* ODE *for Music.*

WHEN Music, Heav'nly Maid, was young,
While yet in early *Greece* she sung,
The Passions oft to hear her Shell,
Throng'd around her magic Cell,
Exulting, trembling, raging, fainting,
Possest beyond the Muse's Painting ;
By turns they felt the glowing Mind,
Disturb'd, delighted, rais'd, refin'd.
Till once, 'tis said, when all were fir'd,
Fill'd with Fury, rapt, inspir'd,   10
From the supporting Myrtles round,
They snatch'd her Instruments of Sound,
And as they oft had heard a-part
Sweet Lessons of her forceful Art,
Each, for Madness rul'd the Hour,
Would prove his own expressive Pow'r.

First *Fear* his Hand, its Skill to try,
  Amid the Chords bewilder'd laid,
And back recoil'd he knew not why,
  Ev'n at the Sound himself had made.   20

Next *Anger* rush'd ; his Eyes on fire
   In Lightnings own'd his secret Stings :
In one rude Clash he struck the Lyre,
   And swept with hurried Hand the Strings.

With woful Measures wan *Despair*
   Low sullen Sounds his Grief beguil'd,
A solemn, strange, and mingled Air,
   'Twas sad by Fits, by Starts 'twas wild.

But thou, O *Hope*, with Eyes so fair,
   What was thy delightful Measure ?   30
Still it whisper'd promis'd Pleasure,
   And bad the lovely Scenes at distance hail !

Still would Her Touch the Strain prolong,
   And from the Rocks, the Woods, the Vale,
She call'd on Echo still thro' all the Song ;
   And, where Her sweetest Theme She chose,
   A soft responsive Voice was heard at ev'ry Close,
And *Hope* enchanted smil'd, and wav'd Her golden Hair.
And longer had She sung,—but with a Frown,
     Revenge impatient rose,   40
He threw his blood-stain'd Sword in Thunder down,
     And with a with'ring Look,
   The War-denouncing Trumpet took,
And blew a Blast so loud and dread,
Were ne'er Prophetic Sounds so full of Woe.

And ever and anon he beat

    The doubling Drum with furious Heat ;

  And tho' sometimes each dreary Pause between,

    Dejected *Pity* at his Side,

    Her Soul-subduing Voice applied,   50

  Yet still He kept his wild unalter'd Mien,

While each strain'd Ball of Sight seem'd bursting from

    his Head.

  Thy Numbers, *Jealousy*, to nought were fix'd,

    Sad Proof of thy distressful State,

  Of diff'ring Themes the veering Song was mix'd,

    And now it courted *Love*, now raving call'd on *Hate*.

With Eyes up-rais'd, as one inspir'd,

Pale *Melancholy* sate retir'd,

And from her wild sequester'd Seat,

In Notes by Distance made more sweet,   60

Pour'd thro' the mellow *Horn* her pensive Soul :

  And dashing soft from Rocks around,

  Bubbling Runnels join'd the Sound ;

Thro' Glades and Glooms the mingled Measure stole,

  Or o'er some haunted Stream with fond Delay,

    Round an holy Calm diffusing,

    Love of Peace, and lonely Musing,

  In hollow Murmurs died away.

But O how alter'd was its sprightlier Tone !

When *Chearfulness*, a Nymph of healthiest Hue, 70
   Her Bow a-cross her Shoulder flung,
   Her Buskins gem'd with Morning Dew,
Blew an inspiring Air, that Dale and Thicket rung,
   The Hunter's Call to *Faun* and *Dryad* known !
   The Oak-crown'd *Sisters*, and their chast-eye'd *Queen*,
   Satyrs and sylvan Boys were seen,
   Peeping from forth their Alleys green ;
Brown *Exercise* rejoic'd to hear,
   And *Sport* leapt up, and seiz'd his Beechen Spear.

Last came *Joy*'s Ecstatic Trial, 80
He with viny Crown advancing,
   First to the lively Pipe his Hand addrest,
But soon he saw the brisk awak'ning Viol,
   Whose sweet entrancing Voice he lov'd the best.
     They would have thought who heard the Strain,
     They saw in *Tempe*'s Vale her native Maids,
     Amidst the festal sounding Shades,
To some unwearied Minstrel dancing,
   While as his flying Fingers kiss'd the Strings, 89
   Love fram'd with *Mirth*, a gay fantastic Round,
   Loose were Her Tresses seen, her Zone unbound,
   And HE amidst his frolic Play,
As if he would the charming Air repay,
Shook thousand Odours from his dewy Wings.

O *Music*, Sphere-descended Maid,
Friend of Pleasure, *Wisdom*'s Aid,
Why, Goddess, why to us deny'd?
Lay'st Thou thy antient Lyre aside?
As in that lov'd *Athenian* Bow'r,
You learn'd an all-commanding Pow'r, 100
Thy mimic Soul, O Nymph endear'd,
Can well recall what then it heard.
Where is thy native simple Heart,
Devote to Virtue, Fancy, Art?
Arise as in that elder Time,
Warm, Energic, Chaste, Sublime!
Thy Wonders in that God-like Age,
Fill thy recording *Sister*'s Page—
'Tis said, and I believe the Tale,
Thy humblest *Reed* could more prevail, 110
Had more of Strength, diviner Rage,
Than all which charms this laggard Age,
Ev'n all at once together found,
Cæcilia's mingled World of Sound—
O bid our vain Endeavors cease,
Revive the just Designs of *Greece*,
Return in all thy simple State!
Confirm the Tales Her Sons relate!

O D E

Occaſion'd by the DEATH of

Mr. *T H O M S O N.*

By Mr. WILLIAM COLLINS.

Hæc tibi ſemper erunt, & cum ſolennia Vota
Reddemus Nymphis, & cum luſtrabimus Agros.

—— —— *Amavit nos quoque Daphnis.*
VIRG. Bucol. Eclog. v.

L O N D O N:

Printed for R. MANBY and H. S. COX, on *Ludgate-Hill.*
MDCCXLIX.

[Price Six-pence.]

TO

GEORGE LYTTLETON, Efq;

THIS

O D E

IS INSCRIB'D BY

The AUTHOR.

ADVERTISEMENT

THE Scene of the following Stanzas is ſuppos'd to lie on the *Thames* near *Richmond.*

O D E

ON THE

Death of Mr. *THOMSON*.

I.

In yonder Grave a Druid lies
   Where slowly winds the stealing Wave !
The *Year*'s best Sweets shall duteous rise
   To deck *it's* Poet'*s* sylvan Grave !

II.

In yon deep Bed of whisp'ring Reeds
   His airy Harp * shall now be laid,
That He, whose Heart in Sorrow bleeds
   May love thro' Life the soothing Shade.

III.

Then Maids and Youths shall linger here,
   And while it's Sounds at distance swell,   10
Shall sadly seem in Pity's Ear
   To hear the Woodland Pilgrim's Knell.

* The Harp of *Æolus*, of which see a Description in the *Castle of Indolence*.

IV.

REMEMBRANCE oft shall haunt the Shore
  When THAMES in Summer-wreaths is drest,
And oft suspend the dashing Oar
  To bid his gentle Spirit rest !

V.

And oft as EASE and HEALTH retire
  To breezy Lawn, or Forest deep,
The Friend shall view yon whit'ning Spire *,
  And 'mid the varied Landscape weep.   20

VI.

But Thou, who own'st that Earthy Bed,
  Ah ! what will ev'ry Dirge avail ?
Or Tears, which LOVE and PITY shed
  That mourn beneath the gliding Sail !

VII.

Yet lives there one, whose heedless Eye
  Shall scorn thy pale Shrine glimm'ring near ?
With Him, Sweet Bard, may FANCY die,
  And JOY desert the blooming Year.

          * *Richmond*-Church.

VIII.

But thou, lorn STREAM, whose sullen Tide
  No sedge-crown'd SISTERS now attend,   30
Now waft me from the green Hill's Side
  Whose cold Turf hides the buried FRIEND !

IX.

And see, the Fairy Valleys fade,
  Dun *Night* has veil'd the solemn View !
—Yet once again, Dear parted SHADE
  Meek NATURE's CHILD again adieu !

X.

The genial Meads assign'd to bless
  Thy Life, shall mourn thy early Doom,
Their Hinds, and Shepherd-Girls shall dress
  With simple Hands thy rural Tomb.   40

XI.

Long, long, thy Stone and pointed Clay
  Shall melt the musing BRITON's Eyes,
O ! VALES, and WILD WOODS, shall HE say
  In yonder Grave YOUR DRUID lies !

A SONG from

Shakespear's CYMBELYNE.

SUNG BY GUIDERUS AND ARVIRAGUS OVER FIDELE,

SUPPOS'D TO BE DEAD.

See page 278 *of the* 7*th Vol. of* THEOBALD's *Edition of* SHAKE-
SPEAR.

[First published in the second and revised edition of the
Epistle to Sir Thomas Hanmer, 1744; reprinted under the title
Elegiac Song, and with alterations by the editor, in the *Gentle-
man's Magazine* for October 1749. It was correctly printed by
Dodsley in the fourth volume of his *Collection*.]

I.

To fair FIDELE's grassy Tomb

Soft Maids, and Village Hinds shall bring

Each op'ning Sweet, of earliest Bloom,

And rifle all the breathing Spring.

II.

No wailing Ghost shall dare appear

To vex with Shrieks this quiet Grove :

But Shepherd Lads assemble here,

And melting Virgins own their Love.

III.

No wither'd Witch shall here be seen,
  No Goblins lead their nightly Crew: 10
The Female Fays shall haunt the Green,
  And dress thy Grave with pearly Dew!

IV.

The Redbreast oft at Ev'ning Hours
  Shall kindly lend his little Aid:
With hoary Moss, and gather'd Flow'rs,
  To deck the Ground where thou art laid.

V.

When howling Winds, and beating Rain,
  In Tempests shake the sylvan Cell:
Or midst the Chace on ev'ry Plain,
  The tender Thought on thee shall dwell.   20

VI.

Each lonely Scene shall thee restore,
  For thee the Tear be duly shed:
Belov'd, till Life could charm no more;
  And mourn'd, till Pity's self be dead.

AN ODE

ON THE POPULAR SUPERSTITIONS OF THE HIGHLANDS OF SCOTLAND,

CONSIDERED AS THE SUBJECT OF POETRY.

[Written about 1749 and first printed with interpolations by the editor in the *Transactions* of the Royal Society of Edinburgh, I. ii, § ii, p. 63.]

H[ome], thou return'st from Thames, whose Naiads long
    Have seen thee ling'ring, with a fond delay,
Mid those soft friends, whose hearts, some future day,
    Shall melt, perhaps, to hear thy tragic song.
Go, not unmindful of that cordial youth,
    Whom, long endear'd, thou leav'st by Lavant's side ;
Together let us wish him lasting truth,
    And joy untainted with his destin'd bride.
Go ! nor regardless, while these numbers boast
    My short-liv'd bliss, forget my social name ;   10
But think far off how, on the southern coast,
    I met thy friendship with an equal flame !
Fresh to that soil thou turn'st, whose ev'ry vale

Shall prompt the poet, and his song demand :
To thee thy copious subjects ne'er shall fail ;
   Thou need'st but take the pencil to thy hand,
And paint what all believe who own thy genial land.

II.

THERE must thou wake perforce thy Doric quill,
   'Tis Fancy's land to which thou sett'st thy feet ;
Where still, 'tis said, the fairy people meet   20
   Beneath each birken shade on mead or hill.
There each trim lass that skims the milky store
   To the swart tribes their creamy bowl allots ;
By night they sip it round the cottage-door,
   While airy minstrels warble jocund notes.
There every herd, by sad experience, knows
   How, wing'd with fate, their elf-shot arrows fly ;
When the sick ewe her summer food foregoes,
   Or, stretch'd on earth, the heart-smit heifers lie.
Such airy beings awe th' untutor'd swain :   30
   Nor thou, though learn'd, his homelier thoughts neglect;
Let thy sweet muse the rural faith sustain :
   These are the themes of simple, sure effect,
That add new conquests to her boundless reign,
   And fill, with double force, her heart-commanding strain.

III.

Ev'n yet preserv'd, how often may'st thou hear,
 Where to the pole the Boreal mountains run,
Taught by the father to his list'ning son
 Strange lays, whose power had charm'd a SPENCER's ear.
At ev'ry pause, before thy mind possest,   40
 Old RUNIC bards shall seem to rise around,
With uncouth lyres, in many-coloured vest,
 Their matted hair with boughs fantastic crown'd :
Whether thou bid'st the well-taught hind repeat
 The choral dirge that mourns some chieftain brave,
When ev'ry shrieking maid her bosom beat,
 And strew'd with choicest herbs his scented grave ;
Or whether, sitting in the shepherd's shiel,
 Thou hear'st some sounding tale of war's alarms ;
When, at the bugle's call, with fire and steel,   50
 The sturdy clans pour'd forth their bony swarms,
And hostile brothers met to prove each other's arms.

IV.

'Tis thine to sing, how framing hideous spells
 In SKY's lone isle the gifted wizzard seer,
Lodged in the wintry cave [his wayward fits],
 Or in the depth of Uist's dark forests dwells :

How they, whose sight such dreary dreams engross,
  With their own visions oft astonish'd droop,
When o'er the wat'ry strath or quaggy moss
  They see the gliding ghosts unbodied troop.   60
Or if in sports, or on the festive green,
  Their [piercing] glance some fated youth descry,
Who, now perhaps in lusty vigour seen
  And rosy health, shall soon lamented die.
For them the viewless forms of air obey,
  Their bidding heed, and at their beck repair.
They know what spirit brews the stormful day,
  And heartless, oft like moody madness stare
To see the phantom train their secret work prepare.

[Stanza V lost.]

VI.

[8 lines lost.]

What though far off, from some dark dell espied
  His glimm'ring mazes cheer th' excursive sight,
Yet turn, ye wand'rers, turn your steps aside,
  Nor trust the guidance of that faithless light;
For watchful, lurking 'mid th' unrustling reed,
  At those mirk hours the wily monster lies,   100
And listens oft to hear the passing steed,
  And frequent round him rolls his sullen eyes,
If chance his savage wrath may some weak wretch surprise.

VII.

Ah, luckless swain, o'er all unblest indeed !
　Whom late bewilder'd in the dank, dark fen,
Far from his flocks and smoking hamlet then !
　To that sad spot [his wayward fate shall lead] :
On him enrag'd, the fiend, in angry mood,
　Shall never look with pity's kind concern,
But instant, furious, raise the whelming flood　　110
　O'er its drown'd bank, forbidding all return.
Or, if he meditate his wish'd escape
　To some dim hill that seems uprising near,
To his faint eye the grim and grisly shape,
　In all its terrors clad, shall wild appear.
Meantime, the wat'ry surge shall around him rise,
　Pour'd sudden forth from ev'ry swelling source.
What now remains but tears and hopeless sighs ?
　His fear-shook limbs have lost their youthly force,
And down the waves he floats, a pale and breathless corse.

VIII.

For him, in vain, his anxious wife shall wait,　　121
　Or wander forth to meet him on his way ;
For him, in vain, at to-fall of the day,
　His babes shall linger at th' unclosing gate !

Ah, ne'er shall he return !   Alone, if night
 Her travell'd limbs in broken slumbers steep,
With dropping willows drest, his mournful sprite
 Shall visit sad, perchance, her silent sleep :
Then he, perhaps, with moist and wat'ry hand,
 Shall fondly seem to press her shudd'ring cheek, 130
And with his blue swoln face before her stand,
 And, shiv'ring cold, these piteous accents speak :
Pursue, dear wife, thy daily toils pursue
 At dawn or dusk, industrious as before ;
Nor e'er of me one hapless thought renew,
 While I lie welt'ring on the ozier'd shore,
Drown'd by the KAELPIE's wrath, nor e'er shall aid thee
  more !

IX.

UNBOUNDED is thy range ;   with varied stile
 Thy muse may, like those feath'ry tribes which spring
From their rude rocks, extend her skirting wing 140
 Round the moist marge of each cold Hebrid isle,
To that hoar pile which still its ruin shows :
 In whose small vaults a pigmy-folk is found,
Whose bones the delver with his spade upthrows,
 And culls them, wond'ring, from the hallow'd ground !

Or thither where beneath the show'ry west
   The mighty kings of three fair realms are laid :
Once foes, perhaps, together now they rest.
   No slaves revere them, and no wars invade :
Yet frequent now, at midnight's solemn hour,   150
   The rifted mounds their yawning cells unfold,
And forth the monarchs stalk with sov'reign pow'r
   In pageant robes, and wreath'd with sheeny gold,
And on their twilight tombs aerial council hold.

x.

But O ! o'er all, forget not KILDA's race,
   On whose bleak rocks, which brave the wasting tides,
Fair Nature's daughter, Virtue, yet abides.
   Go, just, as they, their blameless manners trace !
Then to my ear transmit some gentle song
   Of those whose lives are yet sincere and plain,   160
Their bounded walks the rugged cliffs along,
   And all their prospect but the wintry main.
With sparing temp'rance, at the needful time,
   They drain the sainted spring, or, hunger-prest,
Along th' Atlantic rock undreading climb,
   And of its eggs despoil the Solan's nest.

Thus blest in primal innocence they live,

   Suffic'd and happy with that frugal fare

Which tasteful toil and hourly danger give.

   Hard is their shallow soil, and bleak and bare ;   170

Nor ever vernal bee was heard to murmur there !

XI.

NOR need'st thou blush, that such false themes engage

   Thy gentle mind, of fairer stores possest ;

For not alone they touch the village breast,

   But fill'd in elder time th' historic page.

There SHAKESPEARE's self, with ev'ry garland crown'd,

   In musing hour, his wayward sisters found,

And with their terrors drest the magic scene.

From them he sung, when mid his bold design,

   Before the Scot afflicted and aghast,   180

The shadowy kings of BANQUO's fated line,

   Through the dark cave in gleamy pageant past.

Proceed, nor quit the tales which, simply told,

   Could once so well my answ'ring bosom pierce ;

Proceed, in forceful sounds and colours bold

   The native legends of thy land rehearse ;

To such adapt thy lyre and suit thy powerful verse.

XII.

In scenes like these, which, daring to depart

   From sober truth, are still to nature true,

And call forth fresh delight to fancy's view,   190

   Th' heroic muse employ'd her Tasso's art!

How have I trembled, when at Tancred's stroke,

   Its gushing blood the gaping cypress pour'd;

When each live plant with mortal accents spoke,

   And the wild blast up-heav'd the vanish'd sword!

How have I sat, when pip'd the pensive wind,

   To hear his harp, by British Fairfax strung.

Prevailing poet, whose undoubting mind

   Believ'd the magic wonders which he sung!

Hence at each sound imagination glows;   200

Hence his warm lay with softest sweetness flows;

   Melting it flows, pure, num'rous, strong and clear,

And fills th' impassion'd heart, and wins th' harmonious

     ear.

XIII.

All hail, ye scenes that o'er my soul prevail,

   Ye [spacious] friths and lakes which, far away,

Are by smooth Annan fill'd, or past'ral Tay,

   Or Don's romantic springs, at distance, hail!

The time shall come when I, perhaps, may tread
Your lowly glens, o'erhung with spreading broom,
Or o'er your stretching heaths by fancy led :　　　210
Then will I dress once more the faded bow'r,
Where JOHNSON sat in DRUMMOND's [social] shade;
Or crop from Tiviot's dale each [classic flower],
And mourn on Yarrow's banks [the widow'd maid.]
Meantime, ye Pow'rs, that on the plains which bore
The cordial youth, on LOTHIAN's plains attend,
Where'er he dwell, on hill, or lowly muir,
To him I lose, your kind protection lend,
And, touch'd with love like mine, preserve my absent
friend.

WRITTEN ON A PAPER, WHICH CONTAINED A PIECE OF BRIDE CAKE GIVEN TO THE AUTHOR BY A LADY.

[First published in the *Gentleman's Magazine*, May 1765.]

Ye curious hands, that, hid from vulgar eyes,
　By search profane shall find this hallow'd cake,
With virtue's awe forbear the sacred prize,
　Nor dare a theft for love and pity's sake!

This precious relick, form'd by magick pow'r,
　Beneath her shepherd's haunted pillow laid,
Was meant by love to charm the silent hour,
　The secret present of a matchless maid.

The *Cypryan* queen, at hymen's fond request,
　Each nice ingredient chose with happiest art;　　10
Fears, sighs, and wishes of th' enamoured breast,
　And pains that please, are mixt in every part.

With rosy hand the spicy fruit she brought
   From *Paphian* hills, and fair *Cythera*'s isle;
And tempered sweet with these the melting thought,
   The kiss ambrosial and the yielding smile.

Ambiguous looks, that scorn and yet relent,
   Denials mild, and firm unalter'd truth,
Reluctant pride, and amorous faint consent,
   And meeting ardors and exulting youth.   20

Sleep, wayward God! hath sworn while these remain,
   With flattering dreams to dry his nightly tear,
And chearful *Hope*, so oft invok'd in vain,
   With fairy songs shall soothe his pensive ear.

If bound by vows to friendship's gentle side,
   And fond of soul, thou hop'st an equal grace,
If youth or maid thy joys and griefs divide,
   O much intreated leave this fatal place.

Sweet *Peace*, who long hath shunn'd my plaintive day
   Consents at length to bring me short delight,   30
Thy careless steps may scare her doves away,
   And grief with raven note usurp the night.

SONG.

The Sentiments borrowed from SHAKSPEARE.

[Perhaps written at Winchester in 1739. Printed in the
Gentleman's Magazine, Feb. 1788, and first included among
Collins's works in Johnson's *English Poets*, vol. 58, 1790.]

YOUNG Damon of the vale is dead,
  Ye lowland hamlets moan:
A dewy turf lies o'er his head,
  And at his feet a stone.

His shroud, which death's cold damps destroy,
  Of snow-white threads was made:
All mourn'd to see so sweet a boy
  In earth for ever laid.

Pale pansies o'er his corpse were plac'd,
  Which, pluck'd before their time,   10
Bestrew'd the boy like him to waste,
  And wither in their prime.

X

But will he ne'er return, whose tongue
    Could tune the rural lay ?
Ah, no ! his bell of peace is rung,
    His lips are cold as clay.

They bore him out at twilight hour,
    The youth who lov'd so well :
Ah me ! how many a true-love shower
    Of kind remembrance fell !   20

Each maid was woe—but Lucy chief,
    Her grief o'er all was tried,
Within his grave she dropp'd in grief,
    And o'er her lov'd-one died.

NOTES.

PERSIAN ECLOGUES.

A unique copy of the 1742 edition, containing autograph notes of Collins, is preserved in the Dyce Library at South Kensington. The title-page with the altered motto and the cancelled imprint is reproduced before the text. On the back of the title-page is a note by Joseph Warton: 'Mr. Collins gave me this Copy with his own Hands when I & my Brother visited Him for the Last time at Chichester.' The following corrections are made in the text:

First Eclogue.

17. 'Wand'rer' *is corrected to* '[w]and'ring'. *The initial* 'w' *has been cut off by the binder.* This correction has been made in the text.

In ll. 19, 21, *and* 25 'ye' *is corrected to* 'you'.

These corrections were made in *Oriental Eclogues*, 1757.

Third Eclogue.

The note to l. 15 is cut through, but was not deleted in the second edition.

Fourth Eclogue.

49. 'Seats' *is corrected to* 'tents', *and* l. 51 'Dale' *is corrected to* 'Date'. This last correction has been made in the text.

These corrections were made in *Oriental Eclogues*, 1757.

The Dyce copy is of special interest because it preserves one of the only two examples now known of the poet's handwriting (the other is a letter in the British Museum).

Except where otherwise noted, the following are the variations in the second edition entitled Oriental Eclogues, *1757 :*

PREFACE.

P. 212, l. 3. *Mahamed*] ABDALLAH

6. *the Great Abbas. Footnote :* In the Persian tongue, ABBAS signifieth ' the father of the people '.

12. of the Writing] of Writing

16. Reflections] reflection

17. *Orientals*] Orientials *misprint.*

FIRST ECLOGUE.

8. Nor praise, but such as Truth bestow'd, desir'd :

13. When sweet and blushing, like a virgin bride,

17. Wand'rer] wand'ring

19, 21, 25, 49. ye] you

30–32. Boast but the worth *Balsora's pearls display ;
        Drawn from the deep we own their surface bright,
        But, dark within, they drink no lust'rous light :

46. The fair-eyed Truth] Immortal TRUTH

49. ye, shall *1937*, ye shall *1742*, you shall *1747*

53, 54. Come thou whose thoughts as limpid springs are clear,
        To lead the train, sweet MODESTY appear :

69. Eastern] ancient.

SECOND ECLOGUE.

1. Desart-Waste] boundless waste

83. O ! let me teach my heart to lose its fears,

THIRD ECLOGUE.

After line 4 the following couplet was added in the second edition :
        What time 'tis sweet o'er fields of rice to stray,
        Or scent the breathing maze at setting day ;

15. Junquils] Jonquils

FOURTH ECLOGUE.

49. seats] tents

65. Deserts] desarts

VERSES TO SIR THOMAS HANMER

119–20. *Punctuation from 1744. 1743 has commas before and after* Expressive Picture.

ODE ON THE POETICAL CHARACTER

1. *Collins had a comma after* Regard *here deleted.*

ODE TO MERCY

15. *Collins had a comma after* Pow'r *here deleted.*

ODE TO A LADY ON THE DEATH OF COLONEL ROSS.

Title . . . Colonel Charles Ross *Dodsley's Museum, 1746.*

In Nathan Drake's Gleaner, *vol. iv, no.* 187, 1811, *appeared a posthumous paper of Thomas Warton, said to be reprinted 'from* The Reaper, No. 26 ', 1798 : *it quotes variant readings.*

4. While sunk in grief he strives to tear (Gleaner).

19–24. *The earliest version in Dodsley's* Museum, 1746, *was* :

    Ev'n now, regardful of his Doom,
    Applauding *Honour* haunts his Tomb,
      With shadowy Trophies crown'd :
    Whilst *Freedom's* Form besides her roves
    Majestic, thro' the twilight Groves,
      And calls her Heroes round.

This is the version in The Gleaner, *except that in* 19 *it reads* regardless.

In Dodsley's Collection, 1748 *(second edition), and in Langhorne's edition the fourth stanza is printed thus :*

    O'er him, whose doom thy virtues grieve,
    Aërial forms shall sit at eve
      And bend the pensive head !
    And, falln to save his injur'd land,
    Imperial Honor's awful hand
      Shall point his lonely bed !

31. unknown] untaught *Gleaner.*

37. *The 7th and 8th stanzas are not in Dodsley's Museum or Collection, and, according to Warton, they were not in the manuscript.*

49. a] an *Museum.* If drawn by all a lover's art *Gleaner.*

58. Ev'n humble *H——'s cottag'd Vale. Dodsley's* Museum. *So the* Collection, *printing ' Harting's ' and misprinting ' cottage '.*

ODE TO EVENING.

The following variations appear in Dodsley's Collection *of* 1748 :

2. May hope, chaste Eve, to soothe thy modest ear,

3. brawling] solemn.

10. shriek] shrieks. *Dodsley's* Collection, 1763.

24. Buds] flow'rs.

29–34. Then lead, calm Vot'ress, where some sheety lake
    Cheers the lone heath, or some time-hallow'd pile,
        Or up-land fallows grey
        Reflect it's last cool gleam.
    But when chill blust'ring winds, or driving rain,
    Forbid my willing feet, be mine the hut.

49. So long, sure-found beneath the Sylvan shed.

50. smiling Peace] rose-lip'd Health.

52. love] hymn.

THE MANNERS.

35–6. Tho' Heav'n . . . Has blest *1937*] Thou Heav'n . . . Hast blest *1747.*

49. Tho' *Garrod, 1928*] Thou *1747.*

THE PASSIONS.

21–2. Next Anger rush'd, his Eyes on fire,
    In Lightnings own'd his secret Stings,
1747; here repunctuated.

30. delightful] delighted *Langhorne.*

ODE ON THE DEATH OF MR. THOMSON.

1. grave] grove *in Fawkes' Poetical Calender and Pearch's Collection.*

21. earthy] earthly *in Langhorne's edition.*

A SONG FROM SHAKESPEAR'S 'CYMBELYNE'.

[The variations of the poem as in the *Gentleman's Magazine* of October 1749 are admittedly the work of the editor, Cave. I have not, therefore, considered it necessary to reprint them.]

ODE ON THE POPULAR SUPERSTITIONS OF THE HIGHLANDS OF SCOTLAND.

The words between square brackets are those supplied by Dr. Alexander Carlyle in the Edinburgh edition of 1788.

MSS. variations :

In the MS. seen by T. Warton (Gleaner, no. 187) *the name* Home *was written in full.*

44. repeat] relate.

51. bony] brawny.

56. depth] gloom.

58. astonish'd] afflicted.

66. heed] mark.

100. mirk] sad.

124. th' unclosing] the cottage.

130. Shall seem to press her cold and shudd'ring cheek.

133. Pursue] Proceed.

192–5. How have I trembled, when, at TANCRED's side,
Like him I stalk'd, and all his passions felt ;
When charm'd by ISMEN, through the forest wide,
Bark'd in each plant a talking spirit dwelt !

200–3. Hence, sure to charm, his early numbers flow,
Though strong, yet sweet——
Though faithful, sweet; though strong, of simple kind.
Hence, with each theme, he bids the bosom glow,
While his warm lays an easy passage find,
Pour'd through each inmost nerve, and lull th' harmonious ear.

SONG.

Variations :

2. lowland *1788, Anderson*] lowly *Dyce.*
13. will he] he will *1788 (misprint).*
18. belov'd] who lov'd *Anderson, Dyce.*

APPENDIX I.

AN EPISTLE:

ADDREST TO Sir *THOMAS HANMER*

On his Edition of *Shakespear*'s WORKS.

[*Second edition*, 1744; *reprinted in Dodsley's Collection*, 1755, *vol. iv, pp.* 64–70, *and in subsequent issues; followed by Langhorne and Dyce. The line-numbers are those of the first version, inserted for convenience of comparison with pages* 233–40.]

SIR

WHILE born to bring the Muse's happier Days,
A Patriot's Hand protects a Poet's Lays:
While nurst by you she sees her Myrtles bloom,
Green and unwither'd o'er his honour'd Tomb:
Excuse her Doubts, if yet she fears to tell
What secret Transports in her Bosom swell:
With conscious Awe she hears the Critic's Fame,
And blushing hides her Wreath at *Shakespear*'s Name.   [8]
Hard was the Lot those injur'd Strains endur'd,
Unown'd by Science, and by Years obscur'd:
Fair Fancy wept; and echoing Sighs confest
A fixt Despair in ev'ry tuneful Breast.
Not with more Grief th' afflicted Swains appear
When wintry Winds deform the plenteous Year:
When ling'ring Frosts the ruin'd Seats invade
Where Peace resorted, and the Graces play'd.

Each rising Art by just Gradation moves,   [29]
Toil builds on Toil, and Age on Age improves.
The Muse alone unequal dealt her Rage,
And grac'd with noblest Pomp her earliest Stage.
Preserv'd thro' Time, the speaking Scenes impart
Each changeful Wish of *Phædra*'s tortur'd Heart:

X 2

Or paint the Curse, that mark'd the * *Theban*'s Reign,
A Bed incestuous, and a Father slain.
With kind Concern our pitying Eyes o'erflow,
Trace the sad Tale, and own another's Woe.

To *Rome* remov'd, with Wit secure to please,
The *Comic* Sisters kept their native Ease.   [40]
With jealous Fear declining *Greece* beheld
Her own *Menander*'s Art almost excell'd !
But ev'ry Muse essay'd to raise in vain
Some labour'd Rival of her *Tragic* Strain ;
Ilissus' Laurels, tho' transferr'd with Toil,
Droop'd their fair Leaves, nor knew th' unfriendly Soil.   [46]

As Arts expir'd, resistless Dulness rose ;
Goths, *Priests*, or *Vandals*, - - - - all were Learning's Foes.
Till † *Julius* first recall'd each exil'd Maid,
And *Cosmo* own'd them in th' *Etrurian* Shade :   [49]
Then deeply skill'd in Love's engaging Theme,
The soft *Provencal* pass'd to *Arno*'s Stream :
With graceful Ease the wanton Lyre he strung,
Sweet flow'd the Lays - - - - but Love was all he sung.
The gay Description could not fail to move ;
For, led by Nature, all are Friends to Love.

But Heav'n, still various in its Works, decreed
The perfect Boast of Time should last succeed.
The beauteous Union must appear at length,
Of *Tuscan* Fancy, and *Athenian* Strength :   [60]
One greater Muse *Eliza*'s Reign adorn,
And ev'n a *Shakespear* to her Fame be born !

Yet ah ! so bright her Morning's op'ning Ray,
In vain our *Britain* hop'd an equal Day !

* The *Oedipus* of *Sophocles*.
† *Julius* the Second, the immediate Predecessor of *Leo* the Tenth.

No second Growth the Western Isle could bear,
At once exhausted with too rich a Year.
Too nicely *Johnson* knew the Critic's Part ;
Nature in him was almost lost in Art.
Of softer Mold the gentle *Fletcher* came,
The next in Order, as the next in Name.   [70]
With pleas'd Attention 'midst his Scenes we find
Each glowing Thought, that warms the Female Mind ;
Each melting Sigh, and ev'ry tender Tear,
The Lover's Wishes and the Virgin's Fear.
His * ev'ry strain the *Smiles* and *Graces* own ;
But stronger *Shakespear* felt for *Man* alone :
Drawn by his Pen, our ruder Passions stand
Th' unrival'd Picture of his early Hand.

  † With gradual Steps, and slow, exacter *France*
Saw Art's fair Empire o'er her Shores advance :   [80]
By length of Toil, a bright Perfection knew,
Correctly bold, and just in all she drew.
Till late *Corneille*, with ‡ *Lucan*'s spirit fir'd,
Breath'd the free Strain, as *Rome* and He inspir'd :
And classic Judgment gain'd to sweet *Racine*
The temp'rate Strength of *Maro*'s chaster Line.

  But wilder far the *British* Laurel spread,
And Wreaths less artful crown our Poet's Head.
Yet He alone to ev'ry Scene could give
Th' Historian's Truth, and bid the Manners live.   [90]

  * Their Characters are thus distinguish'd by Mr. *Dryden*.
  † About the Time of *Shakespear*, the Poet *Hardy* was in great
Repute in *France*. He wrote, according to *Fontenelle*, six hundred
Plays. The *French* Poets after him applied themselves in general to
the correct Improvement of the Stage, which was almost totally
disregarded by those of our own Country, *Johnson* excepted.
  ‡ The favourite Author of the Elder *Corneille*.

Wak'd at his Call I view, with glad Surprize,
Majestic Forms of mighty Monarchs rise.
There *Henry*'s Trumpets spread their loud Alarms,
And laurel'd Conquest waits her Hero's Arms.
Here gentler *Edward* claims a pitying Sigh,
Scarce born to Honours, and so soon to die !
Yet shall thy Throne, unhappy Infant, bring
No Beam of Comfort to the guilty King ?
The * Time shall come, when *Glo'ster*'s Heart shall bleed
In Life's last Hours, with Horror of the Deed :   [100]
When dreary Visions shall at last present
Thy vengeful Image, in the midnight Tent :
Thy Hand unseen the secret Death shall bear,
Blunt the weak Sword, and break th' oppressive Spear.

Where'er we turn, by Fancy charm'd, we find
Some sweet Illusion of the cheated Mind.
Oft, wild of Wing, she calls the Soul to rove
With humbler Nature, in the rural Grove ;
Where Swains contented own the quiet Scene,
And twilight Fairies tread the circled Green :   [110]
Drest by her Hand, the Woods and Vallies smile,
And Spring diffusive decks th' *enchanted Isle*.

O more than all in pow'rful Genius blest,
Come, take thine Empire o'er the willing Breast !
Whate'er the Wounds this youthful Heart shall feel,
Thy Songs support me, and thy Morals heal !
There ev'ry Thought the Poet's Warmth may raise,
There native Music dwells in all the Lays.
O might some Verse with happiest Skill persuade
Expressive Picture to adopt thine Aid !   [120]

   * Tempus erit Turno, magno cum optaverit emptum
     Intactum Pallanta, &c.

What wond'rous Draughts might rise from ev'ry Page!
What other *Raphaels* Charm a distant Age!

   Methinks ev'n now I view some free Design,
Where breathing Nature lives in ev'ry Line:
Chast and subdu'd the modest Lights decay,
Steal into Shade, and mildly melt away.
- - - - And see, where * *Anthony* in Tears approv'd,
Guards the pale Relicks of the Chief he lov'd:
O'er the cold Corse the Warrior seems to bend,
Deep sunk in Grief, and mourns his murther'd Friend!
Still as they press, he calls on all around,
Lifts the torn Robe, and points the bleeding Wound.

   But † who is he, whose Brows exalted bear
A Wrath impatient, and a fiercer Air?   [134]
Awake to all that injur'd Worth can feel,
On his own *Rome* he turns th'avenging Steel.
Yet shall not War's insatiate Fury fall,
(So Heav'n ordains it) on the destin'd Wall.
See the fond Mother 'midst the plaintive Train
Hung on his Knees, and prostrate on the Plain!
Touch'd to the Soul, in vain he strives to hide
The Son's Affection, in the *Roman's* Pride:
O'er all the Man conflicting Passions rise,   [143]
Rage grasps the Sword, while *Pity* melts the Eyes.

   Thus, gen'rous Critic, as thy Bard inspires,
The Sister Arts shall nurse their drooping Fires;
Each from his Scenes her Stores alternate bring,
Blend the fair Tints, or wake the vocal String:

    * See the Tragedy of *Julius Cæsar*.
    † *Coriolanus*. See Mr. *Spence's* Dialogues on the *Odyssey*.

Those *Sibyl*-Leaves, the Sport of ev'ry Wind,
(For Poets ever were a careless Kind)   [150]
By thee dispos'd, no farther Toil demand,
But, just to Nature, own thy forming Hand.

    So spread o'er *Greece*, th' harmonious Whole unknown,
Ev'n *Homer*'s Numbers charm'd by Parts alone.
Their own *Ulysses* scarce had wander'd more,
By Winds and Water cast on ev'ry Shore :
When, rais'd by Fate, some former *Hanmer* join'd
Each beauteous Image of the boundless Mind :
And bad, like Thee, his *Athens* ever claim,
A fond Alliance with the Poet's Name.   [160]

APPENDIX II.

In the *London Mercury* for May 1923, under the heading 'Bibliographical Notes and News', Mr. Iolo A. Williams wrote as follows (and he now very kindly permits the inclusion here, with corrections) :

In Dodsley's *Museum* for August 16th, 1746, appeared, anonymously, a song which seems to have the signature of Collins in every line of it. It is this :

A Song. *Imitated from the* Midsummer-Night's Dream of Shakespear. Act II. Scene V.

> Lo here, beneath this hallow'd Shade,
>   Within a Cowslip's Blossom deep,
> The lovely Queen of Elves is laid,
>   May nought disturb her balmy Sleep !
>
> Let not the Snake or baleful Toad
>   Approach the silent Mansion near,
> Or Newt profane the sweet Abode,
>   Or Owl repeat her Orgies here !
>
> No Snail or Worm shall hither come
>   With noxious Filth her Bow'r to stain ;
> Hence be the Beetle's sullen Hum,
>   And Spider's disembowel'd Train.
>
> The love-lorn Nightingale alone
>   Shall thro' *Titania*'s Arbor stray,
> To sooth her Sleep with melting Moan,
>   And lull her with his sweetest Lay.

Before I go further I had better confess that there is one piece of evidence in the way of my attribution of this song to Collins.

Chalmers in 1810 in his edition of the *British Poets* gave the poem to Thomas Warton, and added the note that it was 'authenticated by Dr. [Joseph] Warton's autograph in his copy of the museum *penes me*'. That would seem to be conclusive were it not that the internal evidence (a thing which I usually distrust) is so very strongly in Collins's favour that one wonders whether Chalmers may not have made a mistake. The parallel between the phrase 'the Beetle's sullen Hum' in line 11 and these lines from Collins's *Ode to Evening*,

> Or where the Beetle winds
> His small but sullen Horn,
> As oft he rises 'midst the twilight Path,
> Against the Pilgrim borne in heedless Hum,

is so strong as almost to be convincing, especially when it is remembered that Collins's *Odes* did not appear until December 1746. Moreover, the parallel is not a solitary one. Take the second and third lines of this *Song* and compare with them these two passages :

> Elves
> Who slept in Buds the Day.
> *Ode to Evening*, ll. 22, 23,

and

> His loveliest *Elfin* Queen.
> *Ode on the Poetical Character*, l. 4.

And in the last verse of the *Song* there seems to be an echo of line 118 of the *Epistle to Sir Thomas Hanmer*, 'And melting music find the softest Lays', and a similarity of wording and thought to the passage about the nightingale in lines 16–18 of the *Ode to Simplicity* :

> By her, whose Love-lorn Woe
> In Ev'ning Musings slow
> Sooth'd sweetly sad *Electra*'s Poet's Ear.

I would draw special attention in these lines to the words 'Love-lorn ',[1] ' sooth'd ' and ' sweetly '. There are other less important parellels, and there is, moreover, the fact that Collins is known to have written two adaptations from Shakespeare, which have a great general similarity of style to the *Song* in Dodsley's Museum. I cannot help feeling that Collins wrote the poem, and discarded it because he wanted some of the phrases in it for his *Odes*. But I admit that I do not understand how Joseph Warton came to ' authenticate ' it as his brother's. When the *Song* appeared Thomas Warton was only eighteen years old, and if he did write it he must certainly have known Collins's *Odes* almost by heart before their publication—which is, of course, a possible thing. I should like to add that I have shown this poem to Mr. Christopher Stone, who edited Collins for the Oxford Press, and that he thinks the poem is, on the face of it, much more likely to be by Collins than by Warton.

[1] This was ' Love-born ' in the text of the *Odes*, corrected to ' Love-lorn ' in the Errata.

INDEX OF FIRST LINES.

SET IN GREAT BRITAIN AT THE UNIVERSITY PRESS, OXFORD
AND PRINTED BY THE RIVERSIDE PRESS, EDINBURGH

5.61